AN IDEA OF EUROPE

AN IDEA
OF EUROPE

Richard Hoggart and Douglas Johnson

Chatto & Windus

LONDON

A Channel Four Book

Published in 1987 by
Chatto & Windus Ltd,
30 Bedford Square,
London WC1B 3RP

British Library Cataloguing in Publication Data
Hoggart, Richard
An idea of Europe.
1. Europe – Civilization
I. Title   II. Johnson, Douglas, *1925–*
940   CB203

ISBN 0-7011-3244-2

Photoset in Linotron Sabon by
Rowland Phototypesetting Ltd,
Bury St Edmunds, Suffolk
Printed in Great Britain by
Redwood Burn Ltd,
Trowbridge, Wiltshire

CONTENTS

ACKNOWLEDGEMENTS

We would like to thank John Miller and all his colleagues at TVS for their help and encouragement. We would also like to thank Allegra Huston for her advice, cooperation and patience.

R.H.
D.J.

The publishers are grateful to the following, for permission to reproduce copyright material:

W. H. Auden, *Collected Poems*, London: Faber & Faber Ltd, New York: Random House, Inc.; Lewis Mumford, *The Culture of Cities*, London: Secker & Warburg Ltd, New York: Harcourt Brace Jovanovich, Inc.; George Santayana, *The Life of Reason*, London: Constable & Co. Ltd, New York: Scribner Books Companies, Inc.

PREFACE

Some time ago Richard Hoggart remarked to John Miller of TVS how different Europe begins to look to a European who has been working for the United Nations, who is forced to see Europe from outside: as Africans and Asians see it, as Third World countries see it, as Moslems see it. The psychological and cultural shocks can be considerable.

That conversation was the germ of the seven television programmes called *An Idea of Europe* on which the present book is based, which were made with Douglas Johnson as historical adviser. *An Idea of Europe* is a deliberately understated title. *The Idea of Europe* would have sounded assertive or even prescriptive. *Some Ideas of Europe* would have seemed like a catalogue without a focus. So we chose *An Idea of Europe*, pointing towards one way of seeing Europe in the light of extra-European experiences and in the light of what has been happening in Western Europe over the last thirty years.

What has emerged above all is the sense of Europe as a continent of continuing contrasts and often of continuing paradoxes. Our approach has therefore been more thematic than chronological (although a broad chronological progression exists throughout), with each programme showing the contrasts and paradoxes which have run through European history up to today.

The seven chapters of this book stand in their own right. They are not merely extensions of the television scripts. They follow the general division between the programmes, but they can be read independently of the television series. They are far less personal.

The first two chapters set the scene. They ask questions about the definition of Europe, and they describe the formation of Europe and how Europeans came to dominate the world; they are about all the comings and goings, entrances and exits which have characterised Europe for centuries and which in many ways still do. The three central chapters each pose a contrast: diversity and unity, hierarchy and equality, individuality and community.

The last two chapters look at Europe's position today: over-arched by two superpowers, reaching towards a new unity within herself, not sure of what she stands for except in economic terms, no longer the undisputed leader of the world in power, in ideas or in principles.

The business of filming in many parts of Europe and on both sides of the East/West divide highlighted some of our original ideas and modified others. Western Europe is, visually, a continent of motorways thundering almost all the time with heavy goods traffic, interspersed with restless tourists. It is very easy to move around since (and this is an underestimated achievement of the European Community) most frontier posts now simply wave the casual motorist through. It is a continent of endlessly crisscrossing city-hopping aircraft and fast trains. It is an area in which some of the world's greatest medieval cities still sleep on, nostalgic museum pieces for the harassed new Europeans. More and more satellite discs sweep the sky. Shepherds still follow their flocks on foot all day. And overall there is a greater and more widespread prosperity than ever before.

Eastern Europe is different. Her political system and ideology has so far meant she is less prosperous, less busy, less glossy, less noisy than Western Europe. She marches to a different drum, though there are signs now that the tunes may be coming nearer together, or at least that the Eastern European tune is growing closer to the Western.

But it is the spokesmen from different parts of Eastern Europe who pose the most difficult and insistent questions to the West: What does Western Europe stand for today? Does the West stand for anything other than economic activity and consumerism? What happened to the idea of fraternity?

Similar questions come from spokesmen for territories which were formerly colonised by Western Europe, a Europe they now see as overshadowed by greater political and military powers, a Europe which no longer seems to have a firm hold on the ideas and ideals it once so sedulously promoted and propagated through-out the world.

This book, then, represents a joint effort to enunciate an idea of Europe, and above all the continuing contrasts and paradoxes of Europe, by a modern historian and a literary critic, the former drawing on the scholarship of his profession, the latter on direct working experiences of being European in a more than European context.

Richard Hoggart
Douglas Johnson

Magere Brug, Amsterdam 'Our nature consists in movement. Absolute rest is death' (Blaise Pascal)

1 · THE FRAGILE CONTINENT

It has been said that in 1945, when the mists of battle cleared, a corpse was found lying, naked and despoiled, in a corner of the field. It was the corpse of Europe. Or better, it was the corpse of a particular Europe: the Europe which regarded itself as civilisation personified, the Europe of humanism and the Europe of world domination in religion, science, commerce and manpower. Then in the late 1950s and 1960s another Europe appeared. This was a Europe which put emphasis on unity, on creating a great centre of production, on being modern and progressive, on establishing uniform systems of justice and welfare, on giving an example of international cooperation. This Europe, the Western Europe of the European Community, claims to be more than a continent.

Doubtless these views of the past and the present are exaggerated. But they indicate a modern European characteristic: we are selfconscious about Europe. One is incessantly asked, and one asks in turn, what is Europe?

There are so many Europes. There is the Europe which figured in Greek mythology, centring on Greece and spreading into the three parts of the world which were called Asia, Libya and Europe. There is the Europe of the geographers, a little more than half the size of the USA, and an extension of the much larger continent of Asia – the only continent which can be described as the appendage of another. There is the climatologists' Europe: temperate, without extremes of heat or cold, drought or rain, but with distinct climatic regions – an Atlantic zone bringing depressions, gales and rain but keeping the shores free from ice, a Mediterranean zone bringing a warmer, drier climate; and the continental interior which is subject to the sharper Asiatic temperature contrasts between winter and summer. There is the Europe of the anthropologists, who tell us that all Europeans have light skins (white or Caucasoid), and that as European populations have been subject to many movements it is not possible to talk of any racial sub-groups, and unwise to attach much importance to physical variations: but it is true that in northern Europe people tend to be tall; fair persons are the majority in Scandinavia, the Baltic countries, Germany, the Low Countries, England, Scotland and Ireland; Mediterranean people are usually smaller and darker; eastern Europeans tend to be shortish and medium-coloured. The theologians' Europe is simpler: with the exceptions of certain Moslem remnants in Albania and Yugoslavia and of the Jews who do not occupy determined regions, Europeans are Christian, either Roman Catholic, Protestant or Eastern Orthodox. The Europe of the linguists is one of bewildering complexity; those who talk of fifty European languages are speedily rebuked, as are those who insist that there are only four major language groups – Romance, Germanic, Celtic and Slavic. The considerable number of languages which do not fit easily into these groups (such as Finnish, Estonian and Magyar), or which do not fit in at all (such as Armenian, Basque and Yiddish), is still much smaller than the profusion of dialects.

Thus it is not easy to define what is meant by 'European'. But there are invariably two considerations. One is to stress the variety included in the concept of Europe, and to say that it is this very diversity, both geographical and cultural, which constitutes Europe's richness and strength. The other is to suggest that Europe is not simply a geographical expression, not merely a fixed quantity or a determinate area, but in practice a sort of unity or cultural community to which, at various times in the past and the present, Europeans are conscious of belonging. It may be that this community is diverse, but it has, both then and now, achieved a certain homogeneity. Only European history can explain these assertions, for in Europe past and present are inextricably mingled.

There are three fundamental factors. How short the period of European dominance was, only a few centuries; how fragile the idea of Europe has always been; how limited the habitual European way of looking at the world is, and how particularly limited is the British view.

Historians cannot ignore the geographers: southern Europe looks to the Mediterranean, which is essentially an inland sea, and makes contact with other cultures; northern Europe faces the inward-looking Baltic and has traditionally formed its own culture area; the river Danube forms a gateway through the Transylvanian Alps from Asia Minor to Central Europe; the Atlantic seaboard of the western countries has led them to exploration, conquest and all the economic activities which exploit the sea.

The historians' Europe also represents the movements of people. Invaders who came from the east: Huns in the fifth century, Magyars in the ninth century, Mongols in the thirteenth century, Turks in the fourteenth century. From the eighth century there was a reversal of the process of conquest. From west to east the French pressed against the Flemings and the Germans, the Germans against the Lithuanians and the Slavs, the Lithuanians and the Poles against the Russians and the Russians against the Finns and the Mongols. The Swedes crossed the Baltic, the Italians the Adriatic.

Europe was always a fragile continent, liable to invasion and disruption, a catch-all for different peoples in the early centuries, constantly battered and insecure. For example, in 732 the invading Saracens were stopped by Charles Martel only at Tours in France which, in twentieth-century terms, is just a few hours from the English Channel. The Saracens were a comparatively small force, and it is unlikely that Christendom would have been defeated and Western Europe become Islamic had they won the battle, yet the event was an instance of Moslem penetration. Even when European civilisation was at its most ostentatious and successful at the court of Louis XIV of France and Molière was mocking the Turks in his plays, the Turkish empire was larger, richer and more populated than all the western states put together. The Sultan received ambassadors from all the Christian states and sent his ambassadors to them. It was not until the 1683 siege of Vienna and the defeat of the Turks that the western fear of Islam declined.

These invasions and migrations are the seeds of many of the problems which have beset modern and contemporary Europe. The Flemish-Walloon problem in Belgium, the Franco-German problem in Alsace, Poland's uneasy relations with her German and Russian neighbours, the rivalry between Italians and Yugoslavs, the split between northern and southern Slavs, all have led to conflict. Sometimes the apparently haphazard nature of settlements has given rise to national jokes. In Budapest the story is told of the tribe that was moving out of the east into western Europe; they came to a signpost with two arrows, one pointing north which read 'to Finland', the other pointing south which read 'to Hungary'. Those in the tribe who could read went north, the others south – one way of explaining the curious similarities between the Finnish and Hungarian languages. Other linguistic and religious differences were not so peaceful. Europe was fragile not only because of invasions; it became fragile with the self-destruction of internal wars.

Europe is precarious, divided into nationalisms; yet Europe becomes very powerful and is seen by the rest of the world as some sort of an entity. But does this entity exist? Can one define a sort of identikit European, or a European style, a common set of characteristics?

It has been suggested, by Paul Valéry, that the idea of Europe means Greece, plus Rome, plus Christianity. Not everyone accepts this definition. What, people ask, about Tristan and Isolde, about Faust, about Don Quixote, all figures who are inescapably linked to Europe. But presumably Valéry meant to stress the Greek sense of the importance of the individual and the importance of life in the present; the Roman concept of the state and the law; and the Christian tradition which linked the Church with monarchies and the power of the state.

In historical terms Valéry's definition coincides with the great moments of European history, illustrating the importance of Europe's contacts with the world beyond. Greek history must, in many ways, be seen as a fusion with the Orient. Roman civilisation was fixed in the Mediterranean and integrated parts of Europe, North Africa and Asia Minor. The notion of Christendom, a geographical area linked to a community of peoples, goes back to the Emperor Constantine's granting Christians equal status with other religions (in AD 313) and to the development of the Roman Empire as the land of the true faith. Christendom was confined to parts of Europe only; Spain, the Balkans and almost all of Russia were lost to Christianity. There was rivalry too within Christendom. Rome was in some ways a provincial city, while Constantinople, founded by Constantine in AD 324, became the centre of the powerful Byzantine Empire, straddling the trade routes which linked eastern Europe and Asia. On Christmas Day, AD 800, Charlemagne was crowned by the Pope in Rome as Holy Roman Emperor (ruling over an empire whose frontiers coincided strangely with the frontiers of the original European Economic Community set up by the Treaty of Rome in 1957). There were two capitals; two churches developed within Christendom, causing the rift between western Christianity and eastern, or orthodox, Christianity, which persists to the present day. The notion of a common Christendom received its severest setback when the declining empire of Byzantium was attacked by western European armies. The capture and looting of Constantinople in 1204 was the result of a Crusade; French and Venetian ships, originally assembled to conquer the Holy Land, made instead for the greater wealth of the Byzantine capital. The West thereby showed its indifference to the civilisation that had preserved the Christian faith when Rome was weak, and this indifference was responsible for the final fall of Constantinople to the Turks in 1453.

With Russia conquered by the Mongols, whose successors the Tatar Khans became Moslems, and with the conquest of the Balkans by the Ottoman Turks, the frontiers of western Christianity lay for more than four hundred years along the eastern borders of Poland, through Hungary and Romania down to the Adriatic. A Hungarian monastery claims to have preserved Christianity; the

Poles saw their frontier as the border of Christendom. Possibly the attitudes of Hungarians and Poles towards the West today have been affected by the role which they played then, as it can be argued that there are still traces among the Greeks of the distrust that they felt for the West after the crime of 1204.

Byzantine civilisation spread into Russia when in 988 the Grand Prince of Kiev became a Christian and married the sister of the Byzantine emperor. The art and architecture of Kiev began to find inspiration in Byzantine models. Later, in 1472, Ivan III married the niece of the last Byzantine emperor and proclaimed Russia the head of the Orthodox Church. Moscow took over what was left of Byzantium and, once Russia had shaken off the Tatars, its ruler (who came to call himself the Tsar, a Slavonic form of the word Caesar) regarded himself as the only true Christian ruler. The Catholics and later, even more decidedly, the Protestants were seen in the east as schismatics who had receded from the true faith. Muscovy was Christendom, surrounded by Protestant Swedes, Catholic Poles and infidel Tatars and Turks. Europe was again divided.

If we stick to Valéry's three stages, we must note, first, that with the Greeks came the importance of the individual. The Greek philosophers were pessimistic about the fate of the soul after death; they asserted the quality of life now, the enjoyment of earth, sun and the human body. This humanism has become a tap-root of European democratic thinking, and particularly of the idea of human rights. It has also led to the stress on individualism and isolation which repels many non-Europeans ('We have fallen apart / Into the isolated personal life,' wrote Auden, looking at Europe's later history). Secondly, the Roman concept of the state and the law, administration and organised society, is fundamental to Europe. But such principles are not necessarily accepted by non-European societies, who find them antagonistic to the fluidity of relationships which should remain more important than rules. Thirdly, Christianity brings the monastic tradition, the links between monarchies and other power structures and the Church, symbolised by the great cathedrals of Europe. When the Roman Catholic Church lost its universal power, European Christianity flowered into a great many forms and developed into an enormous profusion of sects and heresies.

One cannot remain with Valéry's three stages of the European idea – Greece, Rome and Christendom. There was certainly a fourth, perhaps more important, stage, which leads to the idea of Europe, rather than to the idea of Christendom: the Enlightenment of the eighteenth century. The Enlightenment came about because of various developments which took place towards the end of the Middle Ages. The rise of the secular and sovereign state, ruled by a mighty prince; the age of discovery and expansion overseas; the great advances in science and learning; perhaps most important of all, the Reformation and the religious wars which followed, breaking up Christendom and destroying the idea that religion could be the main unifying force in human communities – all led to a belief in humanity rather than in dogma. Man became the measure of all things, he should not be humble in the face of the mystery of the universe. Europeans were no longer united by Christendom, but thinking Europeans were united in their self-confidence, their belief in progress, their certainty that men could transform nature as Daniel Defoe's Robinson Crusoe had transformed his island.

The eighteenth century was a period of vital change in other ways too. Populations were getting bigger; trade was increasing in both volume and variety; in many places, especially in Western Europe, industries were growing. Some countries were developing strong centres of government in capitals such as Berlin, Vienna and St Petersburg. Others, such as England and France, were concerned with their colonial territories and devoted considerable efforts to extending and defending them. Still others, such as Holland, Sweden, Poland and Turkey, were growing weaker in comparison with their more powerful neighbours. But common to most European countries during the eighteenth century was a sense of crisis which never completely faded. None of the wars settled things. There was no sense of permanence or stability in any of the European states, and for many of them, as the century drew towards its final decades, the crisis seemed to be coming to a climax.

Take for example the two victors of the important Seven Years War (1756–63), England and Russia, both of whom emerged from the Peace of Paris (1763) obviously stronger. But by 1783 the humiliation of England was plain for all to see. The American

War of Independence, begun in 1776, had virtually ended with
Cornwallis's surrender to Washington at Yorktown in 1781.
France, Spain and Holland went to war with Great Britain and for
a time she lost control of the Channel. Many of the neutral powers
engaged in a league against her, underlining her isolation. The
country was threatened with bankruptcy as an enormous debt
piled up. The suffering of the poor seemed more severe than ever
before. For all these reasons, members of Parliament began to treat
the war as if it were only George III's doing, and insisted on peace
being made. But when by the beginning of 1783 a new Prime
Minister, Lord Shelbourne, had negotiated peace, he was very
unpopular. Politicians, and doubtless public opinion, wanted to
put an end to a seemingly stupid war, but they did not relish
surrender. They did not like to see England relinquishing land, or
rights, which she had earlier gained. The French, for example, were
regaining their fishing rights off Newfoundland, as well as a number
of territories in Africa, India and the West Indies. Spain regained
Minorca. In Britain, it became increasingly difficult to form an
acceptable government. The king talked of abdicating. Observers
on the continent prophesied the end of British power and prestige.
Horace Walpole wrote to a friend, 'You must be happy now,
not to have a son, who would live to grovel in the dregs of
England.'

In December 1783 William Pitt became Prime Minister, but
there seemed no reason why this should be the end of the crisis.
He was only twenty-four years old, and although he bore a famous
name (his father, William Pitt, Earl of Chatham, had led England
during the Seven Years War) it was not thought that his government
would hold. Some people called it 'the mince-pie ministry' because
it was not expected to last beyond Christmas. Pitt had only been
called to office by the will of the king; he did not have a majority
of votes in the House of Commons. He had against him some of
the greatest of the Parliamentary orators. But Pitt was a man of
courage and skill, and had the great advantage of having no
connection with the disasters of the American war. His rivals were
divided. His reputation for honesty was impressive, and he had
ideas of financial and parliamentary reform which seemed much
needed. The very unequalness and drama of his situation appealed

to people and when, amid great excitement, a general election was held in March 1784, Pitt's government was returned. His government lasted for seventeen years.

As for Russia, she had asserted her power in European affairs during the eighteenth century. By the 1780s it was clear that a Russian army could always beat a Turkish one; it was obvious that no treaty or settlement could be made in central Europe to which Russia was not a party; it seemed likely that under the firm domination of Catherine the Great, Russia had put an end to its quarrels and uncertainties over who would rule. Nevertheless Russian power, though great, was founded on a very narrow basis. At a time when the privileges of the nobility were elsewhere being questioned, Catherine reinforced the power of the Russian aristocracy and extended the institution of serfdom among the peasants. A wide gulf opened between the government and the mass of the people, demonstrated in the peasant revolt led by Pugachev (1773–75). The position of the Russian ruler remained precarious; Russia remained a backward country. While at the time of Peter the Great Russia had produced more cast iron than either England or France, now these countries were developing new industrial methods and leaving Russia far behind.

Furthermore Russia was not absolutely superior to Austria or Prussia. Both were rivals, yet both were necessary allies. If Russia expanded in the Baltic, then Prussia was the enemy and Austria an ally; if Russia expanded in the Balkans and the Black Sea, then Austria was the enemy and Prussia the ally. Consequently there was a deadlock between these three powers in eastern Europe. This deadlock could only be removed by the sort of agreement between them which in 1772 led to the first partition of Poland, when that country lost about a third of her territory and nearly a third of her population. Joseph II, who had become the sole ruler of the Habsburg lands in 1780, hoped to acquire Bavaria by a similar agreement, and he had also discussed with Catherine ways whereby the two of them would divide up the Turkish empire. But the Bavarian project failed, and any hope of using Belgium (which then belonged to Austria and was known as the Austrian Netherlands) in an exchange for Bavarian territory was made difficult by a revolt there in 1787. The Turkish project also failed when in 1787 the Turks themselves declared war and started to inflict defeats on both Austrians and Russians. The dangers of the situation grew when Prussia, where Frederick William II had succeeded Frederick the Great in 1786, started to encourage the Swedes to make war on Russia and allied itself with Poland. In eastern Europe there were many complicated rivalries.

However, the greatest crisis of all, and one that was to concern the whole of Europe, took place in France. By the 1780s France had attained its modern frontiers (only Nice and Savoy were to be added in the nineteenth century), but it did not altogether resemble a modern state. Although a monarchy, it would be difficult to say where the powers of the king either began or ended. Some provinces had retained a special kind of independence in the shape of provincial estates, which were assemblies representing the privileges of the local aristocrats. There were twelve *parlements*, headed by the *parlement* of Paris, which also represented privileged classes. Local laws and loyalties still existed – just as there were local variations in the systems of weights and measures – so France looked more like a loose, patchwork assembly of provinces and classes than a uniformly organised state.

Within this framework one must notice a number of developments. The French population grew rapidly. By 1789 France had 26 million inhabitants, and was the most heavily populated European country apart from Russia. This created a great demand for goods of all sorts and in the towns people connected with industry and trade began to grow wealthy and powerful. They found, however, that although they were undoubtedly important it was the aristocracy who enjoyed all the privileges. This growing population also put a strain on the country's agriculture. People who were obliged to buy food found that it cost a great deal. Those who grew food often had only small holdings; once they had made allowance for their own needs and for their obligations to their lord and the Church, they had little or nothing to sell. Of course a great deal depended upon the harvest, and a bad harvest meant that everyone would suffer. The nobleman's income would decrease as he got less from the peasant, the city dweller would go short of food, and people in industry would suffer when there was less money to spend on, say, textiles. The peasant himself would suffer from not having food to sell, or even enough to eat.

It is difficult to explain the French Revolution, and historians reconsider their position as more becomes known. However, one should fix one's attention on certain specific events. The government was short of money. Expenses were rising steadily and the cost of the war against England (1779–1783) was very high. They tried to raise money from noblemen and the clergy, the two classes who paid little in taxes. Eventually the Estates-General, or assembly of the realm, was summoned in May 1789 to review the situation. Meanwhile, an economic slump seems to have occurred from about 1776 onwards, roughly coinciding with the reign of Louis XVI, making the new taxes even more unpopular. And the bad harvests of 1787 and 1788 produced great suffering and resentment. But these factors should not be thought of in isolation. Writers such as Voltaire, and events such as the American War of Independence, had accustomed the educated classes to be critical of all authority, religious or political.

There were several phases in the Revolution. The first was the period following the meeting of the Estates-General during which the lawyers of the Third Estate (the unprivileged part of the nation; the First Estate was the clergy and the Second Estate the nobility) succeeded in establishing control of the Assembly and started to frame a constitution. The second phase is usually associated with the violence of the Paris crowd which on 14 July 1789 captured the fortress of the Bastille. Although this occasion is so famous that 14 July has been made the French national holiday, there were many other acts of violence both before and after, both inside and outside Paris, which were as important. Riots were often against tax collectors or suspected hoarders of food, and they marked the Revolution with the sense that there was no going back, no returning to things as they had been before. After October 1789, when a mob of women demonstrating for cheaper bread marched on the royal palace at Versailles, this violent phase subsided and for the next two years there was comparative calm. A system of government was devised whereby the king should cooperate with an assembly elected by the wealthiest people in the kingdom. As the peasant's obligation to pay dues of various sorts to his lord was abolished, it seemed that by 1790 and 1791 the wealthy classes, together with the bulk of the peasantry, were satisfied. Why, then, did the Revolution continue?

There were two chief reasons. The government still had to find a satisfactory way of organising its finances. Various statesmen tried new forms of taxations; they tried to raise money by loans; they even urged people to give money to the state. But these methods were unsuccessful, such was the condition of the economy. Therefore when the suggestion was made that the property of the Church belonged essentially to the whole nation and that there was nothing to prevent the nation from selling the Church lands, this seemed an excellent way out of the difficulty. The decision, taken early in the Revolution, had serious consequences. Since the wealth of the Church was taken away, the state had to be responsible for the clergy and pay them as if they were ordinary officials. Many clergy, however, refused to accept this system and the Pope condemned it, so most of the clergy and many Catholics became enemies of the Revolution. Since it took time to sell Church property (which was usually bought by prosperous peasants or business speculators) the government decided to issue temporary certificates (*assignats*) based on the security of the lands. These bits of paper began to be treated as money and to circulate as such; the strained government could not resist the temptation to print more and they began to lose their value. Eventually, as the *assignats* declined in value, people became reluctant to exchange goods for them. Prices rose still further and there were shortages. The country could not settle down.

The second reason why the Revolution moved into more violent and dramatic phases was because war broke out against Austria and Prussia in April 1792 and against England in February 1793. Some Frenchmen wanted war because they thought the Revolution had gone too far and the only way of remedying things was through foreign intervention. Other Frenchmen were disturbed by the difficulties of governing the country and hoped that a victorious war would arouse enthusiasm and unify a patriotic population. Doubtless there were others who thought that the Revolution would never be safe in France until the doctrines had spread to other European countries. Still others believed that France would become richer by annexing territories.

What in fact happened was that in 1792 and 1793 foreign armies appeared on French soil. A great effort was made to defeat them. Armies were quickly organised, supplied and rendered enthusiastic; speculators and hoarders of food were punished, prices were controlled, some foodstuffs were rationed. The foreign armies had allies within France: the royal family, aristocrats, Catholics, people from the provinces who objected to being ruled by Paris. These enemies had to be eliminated, so the government began to intervene in every walk of life. People had to answer for their opinions as well as for their actions. The Terror was not a wild massacre. It was a means of hunting out the enemy within France. As Robespierre said, the execution of Louis XVI in January 1793 was a measure of public safety.

The climax of the Revolution came when Maximilien Robespierre and his associates became the effective governing force of France in June 1793. He was not a butcher, but a man of great ideals and determination, and only such a man could have united the various elements of the population and saved France from her enemies. But his very success told against him. By July 1794 the Republic was no longer in danger and Robespierre himself went to the guillotine. The Revolution began to relax.

Until 1799 the government was in the hands of weak and mediocre men. There was always a danger of bankruptcy, always conspiracies and plots. The government became completely dependent upon the army, and it was not surprising that on 9 November 1799 a general, Napoleon Bonaparte, seized power.

The significance of the Revolution was not immediately understood in Europe. In England, where William Pitt was still in power, there was more concern over colonial affairs. Eastern Europe was preoccupied with rivalries. But some people began to get alarmed. In England the propertied classes and the Church took fright; in Germany princes who had lands in eastern France found their right to raise money on these estates abolished; Leopold, who succeeded Joseph II in 1790, was expected to do something to help the French Queen, Marie Antoinette, his sister. But little was done beyond uttering threats and protestations. Eventually, in April 1792, it was the French who declared war on Austria in the hope that a successful war would consolidate the Revolution.

The military campaign against France was leisurely, partly because Austria and Prussia were more concerned with Catherine the Great's invasion of Poland in May 1792. But after the French won the victory at Valmy and went on to invade Belgium, the Austrians were concerned to defend their own territory, not to set things right in France, and they had to accept the second partition of Poland (January 1793) by Prussia and Russia.

When victorious French armies started on a policy of annexation in Belgium, Savoy and the Rhineland, it was the fate of Belgium which alarmed Pitt. England's ally Holland was threatened, and the entrance to the Thames could be controlled by a French fleet operating from the Belgian coast. The execution of Louis XVI gave support to an anti-French policy, but again it was the French who declared war on 1 February.

After 1793, the French were again on the offensive in Belgium and Holland, and occupying the left bank of the Rhine. The eastern sovereigns had wiped Poland off the map at the beginning of 1795 with the Third Partition. But the king of Prussia was disappointed with his share and in April 1795 he made peace with the French.

Carnot decided to launch an offensive against Vienna and he hoped that a small army in Italy, under General Bonaparte, would create a diversion. However, the main attack against Vienna was defeated and it was Bonaparte's brilliant victories in Italy which transformed the situation. In October 1797 he dictated the peace of Campo Formio to the Austrians; the French acquisition of Belgium and the left bank of the Rhine, and the French-created puppet republics in Italy, were recognised.

Bonaparte led an expedition to Egypt in the spring of 1798 as a way of attacking England, his only remaining foe. But although Bonaparte defeated the Ottomans who controlled Egypt, Nelson destroyed the French fleet at Aboukir Bay and Bonaparte, marooned, appeared to be a prisoner. In 1799, in the face of French aggression, Austria and Prussia formed the second coalition and renewed their attack on France. Bonaparte escaped from Egypt and Nelson's fleet, and landed in France on 20 October 1799. For Europe this meant another period of upheaval.

Bonaparte defeated the Austrians at Marengo in Italy (1800) and Moreau defeated them in Germany at Hohenlinden. Bonaparte was the master of Europe. Russia, under the eccentric Tsar Paul (who had succeeded Catherine in 1796), was as ready as Austria to make peace. Even England, as it saw the coalition break up, began to think about terms. In February 1801 Pitt resigned, as the king was not prepared to admit Catholics to Parliament, which Pitt had thought necessary if Ireland was to be united with England. The new Prime Minister, Dr Addington (later Lord Sidmouth), agreed to the Treaty of Amiens in October 1801, whereby England gave up many of her recent conquests, including Cape Colony, Egypt and Malta.

Bonaparte had been very successful. Yet within less than eighteen months he was at war again. He sent officials to Tunis, Tripoli and Constantinople; he sent forces to Mauritius and the West Indies; he redrew the frontiers of Europe and reorganised the state system of Germany; in May 1804 he proclaimed himself Emperor and in December, when the Pope came to Paris to crown him, Napoleon would not let anyone but himself place the crown on his head. He owed it to his own efforts and to no one else. Perhaps it is true to see Napoleon as a man of restless, continuous ambition, but it can also be argued that Napoleon pushed his frontiers onwards for purely defensive reasons. He wanted security for France and he did not believe that the sovereigns of Europe would allow France to exist as a perpetual reminder of the overthrow of monarchy and other old institutions. The English refusal to evacuate Malta, in accordance with the Amiens Treaty, was a sign of this hostility. France therefore had to be exceptionally strong.

It was after 1804 that Napoleon enjoyed some of his greatest triumphs. Once he was convinced that he could not invade England, he moved rapidly against Austria and smashed their army at Austerlitz (1805). He turned against Prussia and shattered their armies at Jena (1806). The Russians were defeated at Friedland (1807). This was perhaps the summit of Napoleon's power. He met the Tsar of Russia on a raft in the middle of the river Niemen, and the sovereigns agreed to divide most of Europe and the Near East between them. Russia agreed to keep out English goods, and Napoleon now believed that if he could prevent England from selling goods anywhere in the continent, England would be made bankrupt while French producers would have an enormous market at their disposal.

But this continental system had to be made perfect. In 1807 Napoleon marched through Spain in order to see that Portugal kept to the rules. The Duke of Wellington landed in Spain with an army, and the French forces found themselves in difficulties. In 1810 the Tsar withdrew from the continental system and Napoleon prepared an expedition against Russia. The difficulties of supply and organisation were too great even for Napoleon, and in December 1812 a large French army perished in a severe winter. After this disaster, the great powers of Europe took heart and decided to attack Napoleon again. In 1813 his forces were defeated at Leipzig. By 1814 enormous allied forces were marching into France from several directions. Napoleon fought a series of brilliant and successful battles, but he could not check the advance. In April he abdicated and was exiled to Elba. The Bourbon Louis XVIII returned to Paris and to the French throne.

In 1814 no one supported Napoleon. Even his marshals and his relations were very ready to abandon him. Some of the areas of France through which he passed were so hostile that for safety's sake he disguised himself as an Austrian lieutenant. Yet less than a year later, in April 1815, Napoleon landed on the French coast near Antibes. There were no supporters with him; he had made no preparations; like a fugitive he took to the mountains. Within three weeks he was again sleeping in the royal palace of the Tuileries. The armies that had been sent against him were cheering him. This was the flight of the eagle, the 'vol d'aigle', flying from church-top to church-top until it came to rest on the towers of Notre Dame.

Did this triumph happen because of the personal magnetism of Napoleon, or because of some fickleness and unreliability in the French people? Perhaps both. But it happened also because Napoleon realised that once the Bourbons had been restored, once the aristocrats who had been living abroad started to come back – people would be frightened that the government would try to put the clock back. They feared that the aristocracy and the Church would regain their privileges, that the old pre-1789 confusions and exasperations would return. But Napoleon's return was to last only for a short time. On 18 June 1815, in spite of early successes, Wellington and the Prussian Blucher defeated him at Waterloo. Napoleon thought of going to America. But instead he was sent to St Helena where, until his death in May 1821, he knew only the discomfort of illness and the bitterness of exile.

1792 to 1815 was a period of upheaval for Europe. Great powers were defeated, ancient royal families overthrown, frontiers removed. But the changes were not only territorial and political. Ideas and sentiments also evolved. The Revolution claimed to represent a new conduct of public affairs, whereby questions that arose between states would be settled according to the wishes and interests of the peoples concerned. Questions were no longer to be regulated by the personal desires of kings or force of arms. The partitions of Poland were examples of the old system; the powers had gone through some hard bargaining among themselves, but they had ignored the very existence of the Polish people. The principles of the Revolution sought to put a stop to this sort of practice.

The nineteenth century was undoubtedly a century of nationalism. That is to say, people began to express themselves in a national way: as Frenchmen, Germans, Italians, Greeks and so on. It has been suggested that the explanation for this is to be found in the French Revolutionary principle that the people should decide.

However, the Revolution hardly stuck to its own principles. Even before Napoleon, French troops were marching into states and annexing them not because the peoples wished to be annexed, but because they were useful to France. Napoleon behaved like any sovereign of earlier times as he partitioned territories and forced their inhabitants to supply him with troops. Perhaps here is another reason for nationalism: the peoples of Europe, as they became determined to throw off French domination, became conscious of their own nationality, conscious of the fact that they were, for example, German.

At the beginning of the wars, people in Germany had thought of the interests of the state in which they lived rather than of the interests of the German nation. Many were frightened of Prussia and were glad when Napoleon defeated the Prussian army. There were German writers who welcomed the Revolution and Napoleon, there were German governments who disapproved of both. But neither had any thought of Germany being a nation. The most important developments in Germany were the reorganisation of Prussia and the economic changes which began in 1810.

The first started immediately after the battle of Jena. In 1807 Stein abolished serfdom and introduced other far-reaching changes. These reforms were continued after 1808 by Hardenberg. All the while, the Minister for War, Scharnhorst, and the Chief of Staff, Gneisenau, were building up an army. The economic change was instigated when Napoleon started to tighten up the continental system to the point of absurdity. He was determined to keep English goods out of the continent; wherever French troops would go, there English goods were to be destroyed. Such a policy could only mean that some Germans began to suffer from French intervention. There was a shortage of goods, prices rose spectacularly, there was all the violence of the confiscation. Perhaps this would not have mattered had Napoleon remained the victor of Austerlitz and Jena. But the campaign of 1812 revealed a broken French army. A German national spirit began to show its hostility to Napoleon all the more when it was known that he could be beaten.

In Italy events were different. Italy was divided up into different states, but the eighteenth century had been a great period for progress. A prolonged peace had allowed considerable growth of the population, which by 1789 had reached about 18 million. This led Italians to discuss the questions of how agriculture should be organised, how industries could be started, how relations between the different states should be regulated. Perhaps some sense of national unity might have emerged from this. Certainly the progress was arrested rather than helped by the French invasion. Napoleon had no long-term plan in Italy. He thought of Italy as a stepping-stone in his career, or as an area where he could distribute lands and titles to members of his family or to some of his favourite officials. He thought of other Italian states, such as Piedmont, as areas which should be annexed so as to strengthen the French frontier. Opposition to Napoleon's policy was local and disorganised. It centred around courts, around hostility to the Church, around the ill-paid civil service and so on. There is not in the opposition any general sense of progress. It seems likely that the French invasions interrupted Italian development rather than encouraged it.

The Spanish reaction to the French invasion in Italy was unique: the nobility, the army, the clergy and the people joined together in bitter anti-French movements from 1808. Perhaps the only similarity is to the Russian reaction to the French invasion of Russia in 1812. It should be remembered that this was the first dangerous invasion of Russia since Charles XII of Sweden attacked Peter the Great. Had Napoleon dared to proclaim the independence of Poland, or had he dared to abolish serfdom and divide the lands up amongst the peasants, then he might have had some measure of success. Instead, the total nature of the war which the Russians waged defeated him. This patriotic war gave the Russian Czar Alexander I (who succeeded Paul in 1801) a sense of security at home, so that he was able to pursue Napoleon across Europe to Paris itself.

But perhaps the greatest question that one must ask about this time is, how could England wage almost continuous war from 1793 to 1815, and come out on the winning side? It was not because of strong leadership. Pitt returned to power in April 1804, but few people would consider him to have been a great war minister. His main interest was in the colonies and his idea of conducting war on the continent was mainly of paying money to his European allies. He was often in ill health and he died in January 1806, at the age of only forty-six. Grenville became Prime Minister for a short time; then came the aged Duke of Portland, followed by Spencer Perceval. When Perceval was assassinated by a madman in 1812, Lord Liverpool succeeded him as Prime Minister and put an end to political confusion by staying in office until 1827. However, although a man of tact and ability, he was a far from inspiring leader.

England's successful resistance depended on three main things. First, England kept control of the seas. Nelson's great victory at Trafalgar in 1805 is justly remembered, and the popular opinion of him as England's national hero was quite justified. England was thus able to trade with her colonies and with America – which leads to the second important factor. England developed her economy in a remarkable way. British textiles enjoyed a boom. Not only did British manufacturers provide the uniforms for many allied countries; even when the French defeated the Russians in 1807, they were wearing British greatcoats. British ironmakers and British farmers alike were responding to the demands that were being made on them. Some people believed that the days when war was an evil had gone for good, and war had become a bringer of prosperity. This was an exaggeration: there were periods of slump, prices were high and taxation was heavy. Yet economic growth continued with speed.

Third, the ideas of Englishmen were successfully guided towards a particular end. From the start there had been an anti-Revolutionary feeling among ordinary people. One of the few important riots during this period was in 1791, when a crowd in Birmingham rioted not in favour of the French Revolution but against Dr Joseph Priestley, a distinguished scientist sympathetic towards the Revolution, whose house and library were burned. This tendency was encouraged by the Church of England and later by all sorts of Nonconformist groups. There was a considerable upsurge of patriotism during the struggle against Napoleon, and it is interesting to see how great was the affection for George III, even after 1810 when he had become permanently mad. There *were* outbreaks of violence – in 1811, for example, the 'Luddite' movements, named after a supposed leader of workers, Ned Ludd, took the form of machine-breaking and worker antagonism to employers. Nevertheless, the unity of England during the wars was not disturbed. It was after 1815, when the economic prosperity of England declined with the end of the wartime boom, that difficulties became most acute and divisions among Englishmen most obvious.

The first peace treaty with the French was signed at Paris in May 1814, and the general task of rearranging the affairs of Europe was reserved for a Congress which was due to meet at Vienna in November. But Napoleon's return from Elba interrupted the Congress, and it was not until after Waterloo that it could return to business. In this Congress all matters were arranged by the representatives of the five great powers: the Tsar and his Chancellor Nesselrode, Metternich for Austria, Hardenberg and Humboldt for Prussia, Castlereagh and Wellington for Great Britain, and Talleyrand for France.

Naturally there were rivalries. Great Britain was anxious that any repetition of French expansion northwards was checked. Austria remained suspicious of Prussian intentions in Germany and Russian ambitions in the Balkans. In the end, however, the victorious nations each acquired territory that they considered valuable. Russia took Finland, some two-thirds of Poland, and Bessarabia in the Balkans; England took Malta, the Ionian Islands, the Cape, Mauritius and a number of West Indian possessions; Prussia acquired Gdansk and Posen, about one-third of Saxony, and the Rhineland, doubling her territory; Austria expanded into the Balkans with the province of Illyria, into Poland with Galicia, and into Italy with the kingdom of Lombardy-Venetia. Sweden acquired Norway, Holland acquired Belgium, Denmark received the German territory of Schleswig-Holstein, and a number of German states (Hanover, Baden, Wurtemburg, Bavaria) were also enlarged.

Some of the problems of the nineteenth century are announced by this treaty. Germany is dominated by the struggle between Prussia and Austria, the Balkans by the rivalry between Austria and Russia. Certain peoples find themselves dominated by foreigners: the Belgians by the Dutch, the Italians by the Austrians, the Poles by the Russians. England is strengthened colonially; Prussia and Russia are strengthened in Europe. France, although reduced in size, does not lose any specifically French territory. She still has good frontiers; she is not threatened by any powerful neighbour; the French have gained the reputation of being a warlike nation. This reputation was to remain for years, while European powers shivered in fear of renewed French attacks. Within France a difficult process of adjustment was made, as she moved from the domination of Europe to a more modest position, increasing domestic divisions, and making her more difficult to govern.

Art, music and literature reflected the difficult and dangerous years which had passed. Both the self-confidence and the frivolity of the eighteenth century were shaken. Painting became more dramatic, music more emotional, literature more serious and self-conscious. There was a revival of religion. History and historians were required to find some explanation for the troubles of revolution and war. Perhaps, too, in 1815, there was a sense of anti-climax. One French writer spoke of the silence in which Napoleon had left the world. A period of glory and exaltation was over, and a period of work and progress had begun.

After the wars Europe entered into an exceptional period of rapid and profound change. Traditional social relations were shaken, hereditary privileges ceased to be taken for granted, age-old beliefs and longstanding values were called into question. Those who were conservative, like those who were liberal, believed in the inevitability of progress, although the former saw this with a certain grim pessimism, opposed to the latter's unfeigned enthusiasm. The slow life of the countryside was challenged by a dynamic, restless urban life; the smoking chimney, the railway track and the messy workers' quarter became symbols for the future. Industrialisation produced a middle class that was determined to extend its rights and to increase its profits. It produced too a working class that was able to make its power felt. Before 1789, or before 1815, Europe had been too diversified and fragmented, and the changes within it too uneven, to provide many common denominators other than those of war and peace. But after 1815, the movement of money, goods, labour, technique, was at odds with boundaries and frontiers. Economic change was international.

In 1870 there occurred an important development. Germany, which had consisted of a number of sovereign states, was united in the German Empire. The British statesman Disraeli claimed that this change was more far-reaching even than the French Revolution. A new element had entered Europe: a powerful state with a fast-growing, successful economy accompanied by political malaise and uncertainty. As a result power politics, an alliance system and militarism came to dominate European politics. Around what was called 'the German problem' two wars took place in which the countries of Europe tore themselves apart.

Europe had distinguished itself in three ways. There was trade, there were towns, there was travel. The trader, the banker, the producer and disburser of goods had gradually become more important than the king, the priest or the seigneur. The town had become the norm and the centre of European life. Travel meant the exploration of the world, the conquest of the rest of the world and the attempt to impose European civilisation and culture upon it. It could not have taken place without merchants, without the mercenary troops who were prepared to go any distance, or without the missionaries purveying a fundamental aspect of European culture.

Monument to Henry the Navigator, Lisbon 'A man must carry a kingdom with him if he would bring home a kingdom' (Dr Johnson)

2 · THE RESTLESS CONTINENT

There was a time when the word 'civilisation' was taken to mean 'European civilisation', or, more precisely, 'Western European civilisation'. This is no longer the case, as some Europeans have long since recognised; Europeans were in fact usually the first to discover and publicise the importance of the many civilisations that have existed without a European connection. But no one can talk about Europe without referring to its dynamism, and without assessing the nature and the extent of this dynamic force. Europe conquered the rest of the world. Europe imposed its mentality, its culture, its economics and its politics upon lands which were far distant and strikingly different from it. Europe was a daring continent. It searched for new lands to conquer. Its inhabitants sought new worlds where they could settle and live. There was a need to find new products and to create new economies. There was the desire to spread what was thought of as the true religion. There was the ambition of imposing European styles of government and society.

Today, one is conscious of the comparatively short time during which Europeans ruled, the colonial period. British rule over the African territory of Uganda, for example, lasted little more than the lifetime of a man. The French protectorate over Morocco lasted fewer years still. But one has only to visit these territories today to find that British and French influences still persist. It has become a game to spot the Ugandan schools where pupils wear uniforms like those in any small English town, or to visit a Moroccan café where the conversation is that of a café on the Boulevard Saint Germain. There are countries far distant from Europe where the pillar-boxes are red and where one drives on the left, or where the day which commemorates the storming of the Bastille on 14 July 1789 is special. North America was colonised in the seventeenth and eighteenth centuries, but if you go to Quebec today you will find small towns and villages which are significantly different from one another. Those where the houses are close to the roads and where one church with a great steeple dominates were colonised by the French. In others, the houses are set back from the roads and have gardens; there are usually several churches, none of which is dominant and some of which have flat roofs rather than steeples. These were colonised by the British, often by the Scots. Then there are small towns or villages where the social life is characterised by regular beer festivals. They were colonised by Germans, coming from Hanover or Hesse.

Today, one is conscious of the tyranny which Europe exercised over other territories. Europeans assumed that they were superior, that they always knew best, that their ways were the only correct and acceptable ways. The French poet Aimé Césaire, who is from the French West Indies, describes the native's position face to face with the dominant European, the *commandant*. I have, says the native, carried on my back the road which the *commandant* has wanted to build, the railway which the *commandant* has wanted to construct. And I have, he says, carried on my back the God of the *commandant*. But Europe has also contributed civilised styles of government to these territories, and since it contributed Christianity to some of these territories there is much to be said for Christianity.

Europeans were daring, ambitious, ready to take risks, confident in themselves. It may be true that some of the writers who have written about European imperialism, such as Kipling and Conrad in English or Fromentin in French, were more than hesitant about Europe's destiny in strange lands, and we can still shiver at what Kipling called 'the growling, flaring creed-drunk city', an India impervious to British administration. It is also true that often there were European politicians who asked by what right Europeans were present and active in these countries beyond the seas. But in general Europeans were convinced that what they were doing was right and natural. It was their mission to conquer and to command.

The first example of this was the Crusades. Between the eleventh and the thirteenth centuries the noblemen of feudal Christendom, sometimes accompanied by peasants and by children, travelled eastwards to rescue the strategic and holy places of Christianity from the Moslem Turks. A vast undisciplined horde, the so-called People's Crusade, wandered through central Europe, many perishing along the way in Hungary, to Constantinople. More organised military columns led by French, Norman, German and Italian knights liberated Jerusalem in 1099. Many Crusaders stayed on in Palestine and built churches, monasteries and castles. But the invasions continued, the Crusaders quarrelled among themselves and looted the territories they were supposed to protect. Crusade followed Crusade; one was led by the three most powerful figures of Christian Europe – Philip Augustus of France, Richard I of England (known as 'Lionheart' because of his bravery), and the Holy Roman Emperor, Frederick Barbarossa. Yet prestigious leaders were not enough. The looting of Constantinople in 1204 dramatically discredited the Crusaders and by the end of the thirteenth century the last Christian stronghold in the Middle East was captured.

Europeans remember the Crusaders because they still see, in their churches, the tombs of knights who served in this papal army of salvation. There are good reasons for remembering them other than for their ideals or their illusions, their squabbles and their greed, or for the massacres of Moslems and Jews which accompanied them. The Crusades were rich with the activity of traders, looking for new and exotic spices such as ginger, pepper, cinnamon and cloves, or for fruits such as figs, dates and raisins.

Europeans learned lessons of comfort as they acquired rugs and carpets to replace straw and rushes on the floor and learned lessons of fashion from silks, brocades, dyes such as henna, and glass mirrors imitated from those that were used in Constantinople. Scientifically, Europeans learned modern numerals from the Arabs, as they learned about astronomy and algebra, about the use of opium as an anaesthetic in surgery, about the secrets of manufacturing paper which could replace traditional parchment. The Arabs had brought much of this knowledge from India and China (it was in 1292 that Marco Polo returned from China with the first accurate accounts of the Orient).

The Crusades had provided a great economic stimulus to Venice, which had for geographical reasons shared in their direction and their conquest. It might have been the example of Venice and other Italian ports which inspired Prince Henry of Portugal to look to the sea and to a merchant fleet for prosperity. Lisbon and the river Tagus became the most important and the most exciting place in Europe in the early fifteenth century as Portuguese ships sailed to Madeira and the Azores and down the west coast of Africa. In 1487 a Portuguese seaman reached the Cape of Good Hope and the age of discovery had begun.

It is sometimes said that the crusading energy moved into these discoveries. If so, it was sustained for a very long time. The Portuguese went east, exploring the eastern coast of Africa, reaching India and eventually China. The Spaniards went west, to the West Indies and to the mainland of America. In 1494 the Portuguese and the Spanish kings signed a treaty which divided the non-Christian world between them, but other nations disputed this claim and only three years later John Cabot sailed west from Bristol and took possession of Newfoundland for England. In 1534 the French mariner Jacques Cartier began his exploration of the St Lawrence river in Canada. The Dutch East India Company, founded in 1602, built up a rich empire in the east. New Amsterdam, which later became New York, was founded by the Dutch in 1626, and in 1652 the first Dutch settlement was made at the Cape of Good Hope.

All this occurred before the industrial revolution took place in Europe. By the mid-seventeenth century Europeans knew the outline of the world except for three areas. These were the polar regions, the interior of Africa and the large expanse that stretches southwards from the East Indies. But even within the world that was known, a great deal of exploration and conquest had still to be done. This was carried out in the subcontinent of India, for example, by the British, who had founded the British East India Company in 1600 and who, in the course of the seventeenth century, had established trading posts at Surat, Madras, Bombay and Calcutta. Russia, having thrown off Tatar domination in 1480, expanded south and east to the Pacific and into the Baltic and, in the eighteenth century, Danish navigators employed by the Russian authorities explored the straits between Russia and Alaska, allowing Russian hunters to penetrate the western coast of North America as far south as San Francisco.

These discoveries unleashed a movement of population from Europe. In 1519 Hernando Cortés and some 600 Spanish companions landed on the Gulf coast of Mexico and discovered the Aztec civilisation, which had roots as ancient as their own. In 1530 Francisco Pizarro voyaged along the Peruvian coastline and with less than 200 men launched his assault on the great Inca empire. The Spaniards knew that they were attacking states which possessed powerful rulers, efficient civil services and legal systems, complex religions and much advanced scientific knowledge. But they coveted the enormous riches of these empires; they were horrified by such indigenous customs as human sacrifice and claimed to represent the only true faith; because they were so few they fought with savage ruthlessness; they profited too from the fact that horses were unknown in the Americas, and from the technology of their firearms and steel weapons.

In the hope of finding similar riches in the north of the continent some Spaniards went into Florida and explored the Mississippi. But it was the English who wanted settlements in this part of the world. The first was in Jamestown, Virginia, in 1607. The most famous was that of the Pilgrim Fathers who sought to escape harassment by the government of James I and landed, in 1620, on the coast of Massachusetts with the idea of starting a self-governing community. More waves of settlers soon followed.

But all these settlements were relatively small. By the middle of the sixteenth century there were probably less than 200,000 Spaniards in America, and a hundred years later there were only scattered handfuls of English settlers, and still fewer French and Dutch. It was the slave trade from Africa to the New World, organised first by the Portuguese and then by other European nations, that from the seventeenth century began to move hundreds of thousands of people. For three centuries this continued, changing the nature of the populations of Brazil and the United States, bringing slaves to work the sugar and cotton plantations. One can still see in Gorée, a small island off Senegal in West Africa, the cells, pens, loading bays and jetties which were used to load Africans who were being sent westward. Africans today want to keep these installations as a symbol of their past servitude and the inhumanity of the Europeans. Undoubtedly, both physically and morally, the slave trade was one of the most extraordinary actions initiated by Europeans.

So the world was on the move before Europe began the process of industrialisation. Indeed, it could be argued that if it had not been for the slave trade, the East India trade, the discovery of gold and diamonds in Brazil (from the end of the seventeenth century) and the fur trade, then the capital which permitted investment in machines would not have been amassed. But with the coming of industrialisation, the tempo of European expansion changes, and the nature of European ideas about Europe develops. Before the mid-eighteenth century, the superiority of European civilisation could not always be forced on non-European cultures. The Sikhs in India could imitate and surpass European military prowess, as could the Turks or the Barbary pirates. Indian shipbuilders could build European-type ships with Indian woods, Chinese merchants and African slave-traders could bargain on equal terms with their European counterparts. But once the European merchants found that they had more to sell than to buy, then the real invasion of Asia, Africa and South America began. Ships broke into the ports of India, Java, China and eventually Japan. European products began to flood the world, as European emigrants began to populate the rest of the globe. It was clear that non-European societies could not make the machinery which was becoming the basis of European society, and that they could not organise the great commercial firms which carried out this trade. It was clear too that non-European societies could not always create the political and legal conditions which this new commerce had to have if it was to prosper. Thus it was that European expansion sometimes took the form of annexation – that is to say, of colonialism.

In 1815, the time of the Congress of Vienna, the continent of Africa, for example, had scarcely any European settlements. The few that existed were coastal. The British were in Sierra Leone; British, Dutch and French forts dotted what was then called the Gold Coast (now Ghana); the Portuguese were in Fernando Po; the British and Dutch were in the Cape. But a hundred years later, in 1914 (to take another date of European significance), one finds the whole of the continent taken over by the countries of Western Europe: by England, France, Germany, Belgium, Portugal, Italy and Spain. There are only two independent African countries, Ethiopia (which Italy failed to conquer in 1896 but which was to be conquered by Mussolini in 1935) and Liberia (which was established by American missionary influence). In Oceania the picture is the same. Many Asian countries are conquered, such as India, Burma, Indo-China, while others retain titular independence but receive strong western European influences, like China (from 1842 particularly), Japan (after 1854) and Siam (after 1855). If the countries of Latin America have thrown off their Spanish and Portuguese tutelage, they are subject to the influence, both economic and political, not only of the United States but also of such countries as Britain and Germany.

The expansion of Europe is thus political and administrative; it is also economic, in terms of commerce and investment, and can be seen in the control of commodities such as vegetable oils, rubber, cotton, sugar, coffee, tea, ivory, diamonds, gold, crude oil and others; furthermore, it is an expansion of population. Between 1870 and 1914, a short period of time, 34 million people emigrated from Europe, and before 1939 it was said that a quarter of the people of European origin lived outside Europe. And it was an ideological expansion, as European religions were propagated by the missionaries, so that in 1914 there were 2 million Catholics and 1.5 million Protestants in Africa.

All this came to be taken for granted by Europeans. Everyone in England drank tea as the national drink, although it came from India, Ceylon and China. Everyone in Europe readily accepted coffee and chocolate. National habits were formed around commodities which came from distant countries, so that in the north of England no one would have thought of making apple pie without cloves, and throughout the land a cup of cocoa before bed was as natural as fish and chips. In France the wine that was commonly drunk came from Algeria, while Indo-Chinese and North African cooking became fashionable.

Young Frenchmen were called up and left their villages in Picardy or Brittany to see service in the French empire. Young Englishmen going to grammar schools were advised to study classics and then to sit the examination for the Indian Civil Service. Italians were told that their future lay in Cyrenaica and in Tripolitania, whilst Belgians were offered a quick fortune in the Congo and Germans were urged to take advantage of their opportunities in Brazil or in the Pacific. Everywhere there was emigration. Sometimes this was because of a feeling that Europe was overpopulated, and the landless younger sons, or the politically rebellious, or the religiously dissident decided to leave. Sometimes a soldier, a merchant or a civil servant found that he could succeed overseas in a manner which he could not expect at home. Sometimes there was little alternative, as when in 1870 the French in Alsace were taken over by the Germans and found it more attractive to go to Algeria. Sometimes the inadequacies of Europe were the cause, when the Irish, decimated by famine, emigrated to the United States and the Italians from the poverty-stricken south escaped to the Argentine and to the United States. Europeans would be brought up to believe that they had a rich uncle in Australia, that their cousin was an important person 'aux colonies', that some prominent American came originally from their family, that their friend at school who had not seemed too bright had been successful in Rio or Hong Kong or Madagascar.

And there were always the missionaries. In many ways they were the closest link between the expansion of Europe and the ordinary people. In the Presbyterian churches of Scotland, or in the chapels and meeting houses of Nonconformist England, congregations knew that it was their pennies which sustained the work of their church in what would otherwise have been heathen lands. Some-time letters would be read out to the congregation, or the mission-aries would return on leave to recount their experiences. It was common for schools to receive visits from missionaries, who would often give lantern lectures about their activities. As the old hymns were sung one knew that they were being sung in some exotic land.

In France, the white fathers who worked in the desert had a high reputation, but there were many nuns who worked in hospitals, fighting against the leprosy which was common in many parts of French Equatorial Africa. Small notices appeared in French churches about this work and prayers were said for those who were involved in it. German and Swiss pastors carried out similar roles to their English counterparts.

With the missionaries there is the sense of giving rather than taking. It was easy to mock the missionaries and their supporters at home, as Dickens did or as anti-clerical Frenchmen did, but the mission school and the missionary's medicine chest were important to many. Modern African leaders do not despise the mission schools where many of them first experienced education and in-struction. Straw houses built on stilts in Fiji still contain photo-graphs of the son who went to a Methodist college and became a minister.

Yet the missionaries must also be seen as a disruptive force. They believed that if they were to succeed, the native population had to have a direct knowledge and acceptance of the Christian God through the Christian writings. As an American Baptist put it, 'To establish the Gospel among any people, they must have Bibles. Therefore they must have the art of making Bibles and the money to buy them. They must be able to read the Bible and this implies instruction.' Missionaries coming from a Europe which was wit-nessing railways, gas lighting and mass consumerism associated such 'temporal blessings' with Christian civilisation. If Christianity was to be successful in Africa or in the Pacific, then these develop-ments would have to be introduced there too. Thus Christianity had to be more than membership of a Church. It meant the adoption of a new civilisation, and it was best to begin this in a small way. English missionaries insisted upon the singing of English hymns, the wearing of English clothes, on Sunday observance, on playing English games, on respecting the Great White Queen. They regarded a tea party as a token of civilisation. French missionaries spoke of the greatness of France's national history, of 'la France' and its privileged position in the Catholic Church. The Germans tried to create the atmosphere of a small German town, with its disciplined respectability, its acceptance of authority and its veneration for the king or emperor.

But imperialism is also about power. It was because of expansion overseas, because of trade, because of intervention in the affairs of non-European states that European states achieved world status. Most of them within the European context were small: Portugal, England, the Low Countries, Belgium. France – defeated at Waterloo, then defeated by Prussia in 1870 and confronted by a powerful and united Germany – sought refuge and compensation in an empire which dominated Africa and Madagascar, and which stretched from Central America and the West Indies to Indo-China and the Pacific. Germany had the same frontiers in 1870 as in 1914, but by the later date most German trade took place outside Europe; Germany was a world power, and its government did not hesitate to behave as such. Italy, recently united and conscious of the need to unite Italians, sought to do so by acquiring an empire which would enable her to break out of the landlocked Mediterranean.

All this meant power, and the romance of power. There were some politicians who attacked imperialism and claimed that overseas interests did not represent the true interests of their nations: Lloyd George said that he did not want to hear about an empire on which the sun never set when he knew homes in England where the sun never rose; the French poet Déroulède complained that he had lost two children (Alsace and Lorraine) and he had been offered twenty servants (the colonies); Bismarck stated that he was not a colonial man; Italian workers sabotaged the trains which were taking material for the conquest of Abyssinia in 1895. These instances were untypical. At Jubilees and Coronations British people cheered the magnificent Indian regiments and the Canadian Mounted Police; at prestigious Expositions Coloniales and on successive Fourteenth of July celebrations the French were proud of the Foreign Legion, the Spahis and the gigantic Touareg from the desert who wore mauve veils. The Belgians and the Dutch were always reminded of the immense territories and vast populations which they controlled in the Congo and in Indonesia. A clerk sitting in a dull office in London or Brussels could feel that he was at the centre of a vast, exotic empire. Schoolchildren could contemplate the coloured areas on the maps which supposedly belonged to them. The comforting sense of superiority grew. This was not necessarily accompanied by a clear sense of the inherent inferiority of non-European peoples. Not everyone would have agreed with the British explorer Sir Richard Burton that the African could not develop beyond a certain point, and that he was unaware that there was anything in life but 'drumming and dancing, talking and singing, drinking and killing'. But in the middle of the nineteenth century, there were some anthropologists who believed that certain races, such as the Africans, were in a permanent state of inferiority.

This sense of superiority had its good side. Many European administrators were dedicated men, determined to do a good job. They brought to their tasks a professionalism which remains impressive today. It is remarkable to think that young men – English, French, Belgian, Italian, German – fresh from their education, went out and governed vast areas of territory, dispensed justice over a great variety of subjects, took instant decisions which affected hundreds of thousands of people. And that, on the whole, many of them seem to have done a good job. A code of conduct grew up, officials became attached emotionally to the territories and to the peoples that they ruled. The imperialists claimed that they were bringing to these populations the blessings of civilisation, freedom and peace.

Naturally, this can be depicted as arrogance and paternalism. There were scandals, particularly, it must be said, affecting the German and the Belgian colonial administrations. But the great complaint was that in many territories there was little or no development.

The truth is that in the impact of empire upon the rest of the world, there were success stories and there were stories of failure. In 1820, for example, Tasmania had a population of five and a half thousand, mainly convicts. It was an immobile prison farm, which also held a number of aborigines. But thirty years later the population is 60,000, most of them free. The economy became dynamic, the sealing and whaling industries accumulated capital, the shipbuilding yards were thriving, Tasmanian wheat supplied Australia. In 1848 a Durham prize bull was introduced to the Argentine. Other short-horns were introduced, land was fenced, and the age of the cattle king began. In 1876 a French scientist named Tellier fitted out a small ship with iceboxes and sailed from Buenos Aires to Europe. By the end of the century there were 278 refrigerator ships running from the Argentine to Britain alone. Many of the British working class could sit down every Sunday midday to a great cut of Argentinian beef, bought cheaply the day before; the Argentine became the greatest exporter of surplus food in the world.

A Scotsman called Thomas Glover went to Japan, and settled in Nagasaki in the 1860s. He opened up a coal mine, he started shipbuilding; he built a steam engine and railway; in 1871 he founded Japan's first mint. There were other Britons and Americans who similarly played their part in assisting Japan from backwardness to technological supremacy.

But what of other countries? The Nigerian leader Dr Azikiwe asked questions in 1949, after many years of colonial government. 'Where are the secondary schools, how many of our roads are tarred, how many of our towns have postal and telegraph systems, how many have pipe-borne water supplies, how many have electricity undertakings?' When large territories like the Belgian Congo or French Algeria approached independence, it was asked how they could exist independently since they had been reduced and degraded by the experience of colonialism. Behind the flags and the roll-call of imperialism it appeared that there was a world of misery, poverty and starvation. The benefits of European expansion had gone to Europeans, who had made fortunes in commerce, careers in administration, found glory in soldiery, peace of mind in the missions. Europeans too had drunk the coffee and the tea, eaten the chocolate, used the ivory for their pianos and billiard balls, enjoyed the early fruit and the tinned vegetables, luxuriated in the palmolive soap.

This is why Europeans have a guilt complex about their empires, made all the worse because, since they have decolonised, the difference between standards of living in Europe and in what one now calls the Third World has increased. Whatever the present economic difficulties in some European countries, they are in general set in a pattern of continuing economic development, with rich countries becoming richer. There is thus an encounter not only between the underdeveloped state (in which the focus of life is centred upon subsistence) and the well-equipped state, but also with what has been called the overdeveloped state, where the standard of living dominates the style of life, and where the economic emphasis is on over-consumption and waste.

Europeans try to work off this guilt complex by charity. There are overseas aid schemes; young people volunteer to work in poverty-stricken countries; there are still devoted doctors, nurses and missionaries; there are the Oxfam shops; Bob Geldof and others prod our consciences via our purses. This is the guilt-inspired Elastoplast with which we protect ourselves. Many Europeans too have become reluctant to accept the idea that their culture was always supreme and, especially since decolonisation, they have studied and praised the achievements of the cultures which had been subjugated, and they believe that they must have debased the longstanding cultural attitudes of those whom they once ruled and influenced. Thus we study and admire the art of China and Japan as we collect the masks and bronzes of tropical Africa, interest ourselves in the sculpture and painting of the Eskimos and Red Indians, and are amazed by the achievements of the Mayas and Incas. We talk of the spiritual values of Africa, India and China. In an organisation such as UNESCO, Europeans are only too anxious to preserve the non-European customs and traditions which their forebears did so much to destroy or to distort. If a spokesman from Mali comments that when an old man dies in one of their villages a shelf-ful of books on Mali history is lost for ever, Europeans respond with emotion. Mali history must be protected and preserved, everyone agrees.

It is not always easy for Europeans to help the states of the Third World. Advice is proffered and the Third World spokesman angrily replies, 'Leave us alone to make our own mistakes, as you did.' Nor has everything changed. European manufacturers do good business when they buy raw materials at low prices and sell goods at high prices (including arms). European bankers lend money advantageously. European culture continues to be effortlessly 'superior' as it floods the Third World with Western ways of seeing and understanding, controlling the mass media through cheap print and cheap television programmes. The West can reply that the Third World is not forced to buy the programmes and that if it imposed checks this would be a severe restriction of freedom and one which could have sinister implications. Western Europe was guilty of colonialism, and is now accused of neo-colonialism. The West was accused of cultural arrogance; now it is attacked as the source of cultural pollution. It is said that there is one last bastion of European colonialism still surviving in Africa: South Africa, where those of European stock are fighting to preserve the land which they believe was given to them by God. It is said that there is one last bastion of European colonialism surviving in the Middle East: Israel, where the Jews, mainly of European descent, also invoke God's will. Both echo the Spanish conquistadores of the sixteenth century who believed that God wished them to displace the civilisations they had discovered in America and to govern that land.

The halls of the United Nations have echoed to a debate about post-colonialism. The developing countries have demanded a new economic order, one which would prevent the developed world's exploitation of raw materials, one which would stop the process whereby the rich get richer and the poor get poorer. As borrowing countries find it increasingly difficult to pay the interest on their loans from wealthier countries, and as the prices of many raw materials have slumped, the demand for this new economic order is likely to become more strident.

But new things have happened. The great waves of emigration which sent Europeans to America (and which have caused the Argentinian writer Borges to say that Canadians, Americans and Argentinians are all Europeans in exile), North Africa, Australasia and elsewhere have been repeated and reversed. The process of exits and entrances now brings millions from the West Indies, Africa, the Indian subcontinent and the Far East to settle in Western Europe. The former imperialist powers – Britain, France and the

Netherlands especially – have received card-carrying citizens from their former colonies. Other ex-imperial powers such as West Germany, or non-imperialist states such as Switzerland, receive immigrants (known as 'guest workers') from poorer countries such as Spain, Portugal and Turkey.

Another development is tourism. Europeans can now take cheap holidays in what were once exotic and even dangerous outposts. Visiting the pyramids was always a pastime for a select body of Europeans, but now all the ruins, cave paintings, bazaars, deserts, mosques, temples, game reserves and beaches are within the reach of a package tour. Once again Europeans are regarded with resentment, as hedonistic tourists insist upon European-style hotels and food, and debase and commercialise local cultural traditions (one party of British tourists staying in Sierra Leone, only discovered by chance that they were in Africa and not in Spain as they had thought). But Europeans are also welcome because they bring trade and foreign currency to areas which are otherwise barren of economic progress.

Thus Europe lives with its expansionist past. It is of course a matter for nostalgia, as military museums record the courageous deeds of the soldiers who served in the outposts of empire, as local historians recall how British workers manufactured locomotives which were exported throughout the world, as Frenchmen recall the *lycée français* in Saigon, as Dutch and Belgians remember with wonderment how their tiny countries and small populations were responsible for governing such extensive and distant territories. It is as if we still think of things in the way in which Conrad described the Congo, 'an exotic immensity ruled by an august Benevolence'. But Europeans, in their admiration for their own achievements, in the guilt that they may feel for their excesses, seek to explain and understand what happened. Was their inventiveness simply a stroke of luck? When a German botanist, Burmeister, writing in 1865, was painfully impressed by what he called 'the spirit of restless selfishness' that prevailed among the vegetation of the tropical forest, and suggested that 'the softness, earnestness and repose of European woodland scenery might explain the superior moral character of the European nations,' was he talking unmitigated nonsense?

The effects of this past on present-day Europe are intangible. Some people believe that the National Health Service in Britain took the form that it did because of our colonial heritage, that it was conceived as an authoritarian system with the general practitioner playing the role of a district officer. Today's French determination to play an obviously dominant role in world affairs, the Belgian and Dutch commitment to Europe: these are readily explicable as alternatives to colonialism. When there are race riots in Brixton, do the young blacks think of the slave trade? When North Africans protest about racialism in France, or Moluccans hijack a train in Holland, or Turks protest about their living conditions in West Germany, are their actions tinged by recollections of past exploitation and conflict? These are long shadows on Europe today.

A different kind of shadow is cast by Japan. In the sixteenth century Portugal sent missionaries and merchants to Japan. At first they were welcomed. But as time went by the atmosphere changed. Missionaries were expelled; Japanese who had been converted to Christianity were persecuted. From 1639 to 1854 Japan became a closed country, although Dutch settlers were allowed to maintain a small trading post on the island of Dejima, from which some Japanese scholars acquired books on medicine and science. However, when the American Commander Perry forced the Japanese to accept outsiders in 1854, and when in the following years gunboat diplomacy was successfully used against elements of Japanese resistance by the British, American, French and Dutch fleets, then the Japanese responded with a remarkable acceptance of everything that was Western.

Their army was modelled on France and Germany, their navy on Britain. The constitution was an imitation of the German constitution of 1871, the Civil and Criminal Codes were inspired by those of France. Even if wearing traditional Japanese dress, it was customary to have some Western-style object, such as a bowler hat for men or long gloves for women. It was not only Japanese industrialists and businessmen who imitated Europe: Japanese artists brought such styles as fauvism, cubism and futurism to their pictures. The American architect Frank Lloyd Wright visited Japan in 1916 and built the Imperial Hotel in Tokyo. This was one of the few buildings which withstood the earthquake of 1923, and it gave rise to a school of Japanese architects working in the European manner.

If, in the 1930s, Japan became hostile to the West (though it can be argued that Japanese fascism was an imitation of the West), another period when the West became popular, and something to be imitated, came after the collapse and surrender of the Japanese government in 1945. The American occupation of Japan from 1945 to 1952 was the only period in Japanese history when Japan was under foreign rule. But the foreign 'invaders' were made welcome and Japan embarked upon a programme of industrialis-ation and modernisation which has aroused the admiration of the world. The rise of the Japanese phoenix from the ashes is one of the most spectacular events in modern history. Now the West – the United States and Europe – feels threatened by Japanese competition, and many attempts are made to restrict Japanese sales. Yet the fact remains that this compact country with a remarkable linguistic, ethnic and religious homogeneity has always operated from its home base. If the story of Europe is one where Europeans settled in all parts of the world, there has been virtually no export of entrepreneurial talent from Japan. Nor has the world been flooded by Japanese missionaries or political refugees. The Japanese have excelled at receiving and adapting ideas and tech-niques fiom abroad, and even in music there are Japanese composers who have studied Western music styles and who, like Ichiro Nodaira or Toshi Ichiyanagi, have contributed to the Euro-pean avant-garde tradition. But the Japanese remain at home. They combine their successful internationalism with a persistent refusal to become settlers. The history of Japan is, in this respect, in striking contrast to that of the restless continent.

Kirchstetten, Austria
'If it form the one landscape that we the inconstant ones
Are consistently homesick for . . .' (W. H. Auden)

3 · THE CONTRADICTORY CONTINENT

It is in some ways easy to talk about the unity of Europe. If you travel from Ireland to Poland, you can argue that you are passing through an area of some 200 million people which are brought together by a common heritage and a common sense of values. It is said that the European, and therefore Europe, has been in existence for a long time, because there is a shared consciousness among Europeans which outweighs the consciousness of those things that divide them. The European, confronted with the world beyond Europe, is aware of a real difference of experience. This is to say that the European faced with, say, Islam, or African tribalism, or the societies of the Indian subcontinent, or Southeast Asia, feels instinctively European. But what about North America? What about Russia? What about all the divergences and differences that exist within the geographical area of Europe itself? The German historian Ranke wrote of the unity of the Romano-Germanic people who made up Europe. He wrote also of their diversity, belonging to some half dozen units – French, Spanish, Italian, German, English and Scandinavian – if not more. It can be claimed that nowhere on earth is there a richer multiplicity than within the geographic limitations of Europe, not even among the teeming millions of India or the kaleidoscopic variety of Latin America.

The first thing that strikes us is a bewildering variety. We can contrast Italy to the Netherlands. Italy has natural frontiers; three sides are fronted by the sea and the fourth is dominated by the long chain of the Alps. The Netherlands was manufactured as a state – heroically – before it became a geographical reality or a nation. But there is still a confusion about Italy: not so much, these days, in terms of frontier ambiguities (Corsica and Nice are traditionally claimed from the French, Malta was once claimed from Britain, and various territories are disputed with Yugoslavia), but rather in the differences and the animosities that exist among its component regions. These regions have maintained certain individual customs, in land-tenure, dialect or literature. The great divide remains between the north and the south. By reason of climate and history the southern regions of Italy and Sicily have little in common with areas of the north. It has often been said that the peasant from Calabria has no understanding of the peasant from Piedmont. For him a town such as Turin is as distant and alien as Paris or London; the same can be said of the inhabitants of Naples and Palermo. Countless Italian films show the inhabitants of the south still living in squalor, vulnerable to the natural disasters of drought and earthquakes. Cavour, the creator of unified Italy, never travelled south of Florence. Mussolini, who claimed to represent the whole of united Italy, only visited Sicily three times in his twenty-one years of rule. In 1937 he was astonished to find that a shantytown, dating from the earthquake of 1908, still existed around Messina, and it was only then that he promised to do anything about it. In 1943 Marshal Badoglio announced on the radio that the fascist regime had collapsed, but many Italians resented his Piedmontese accent more than they appreciated the significance of his news. The national language of most Italians is no longer dialect, and with the Common Market and the development of trade with North Africa much in Italy has changed. But it remains a country of variety and parochialism. Even when Sicily ceases to be a region of emigration, it will remain different from the rest of the country, as is Sardinia, and Venice, and Tuscany.

It is not surprising that the same occurs in France. It has often been said that France means diversity and General de Gaulle is reported to have asked how one would govern a country which produced three hundred different types of cheese. There is little in common between a peasant farming the rich lands of Normandy (where it is said that if you drop your walking stick at night, the grass will have already grown over it when you look for it in the morning) and a farmer in the heartbreaking lands south of the river Loire. Bretons living in an arid land by the sea, and sometimes speaking a different language, are far removed from those from Alsace, who are turned towards the European land mass. It used to be claimed that after Paris, the rest of France was a desert. Now that other towns, like Lyons, Rouen, and Nancy, have developed, there are urban regions surrounded by several deserts. Urban against rural, Catholic against anti-clerical, Parisian against provincial, even these divisions have become more complex. If we contrast the northern Frenchman with the southerner, for example, we have also to contrast Marseilles, where the atmosphere is supposedly exuberant, with another southern town such as Nîmes, largely Protestant, introverted, with a reputation for gravity and sadness.

In England the diversity is often expressed in terms of accent. Sixty years ago, a short journey across the Pennines, no more than 1500 feet high, would have taken the traveller from Yorkshire to Lancashire into a different world. The people spoke differently, the corner shop looked different, the names of the fish sold in the fish and chip shops were not all the same. In many Lancashire industrial towns you could tell which of the schoolchildren lived in outlying villages, because they spoke differently from the urban children, even though they lived a mere five miles away.

The influence of radio and television, dominated by what used to be called the BBC accent, is supposed to have ironed out these differences, just as the supermarkets have removed most of the local shops and their specific character. But during the last war, when the BBC decided to invite a Yorkshireman with a Yorkshire accent, Wilfred Pickles, to read the news bulletins in order to emphasise the popular aspect of the war effort, they found that people did not believe the news, or take it seriously, and the experiment had to be abandoned. It could be that the same would happen again. Yorkshire accents are for comedians not newsreaders, just as West Country accents are for cricket and gardening programmes. This is not simply a matter of regionalism; it is a matter of class distinction. George Orwell talked of British people being branded on the tongue, and it is probably true that while all European countries are aware of provincial accents, it is Britain which most markedly possesses class-defined accents. There are certain accents which tell against success. People who leave their regions for the prosperous southeast tend to lose the most prominent aspect of their accent while keeping what they, perhaps subconsciously, think of as less evident accents. Phoneticians tell us that people from the north, living in the south, will stop pronouncing the word 'butter' as 'booter', but will continue to say the word 'glass' with a short 'a'. Since accents have been given class gradings there are subgradings within the accents.

Other European countries know their internal divisions. In Belgium there is the old linguistic and cultural dispute between Flemings and Walloons. It is intensified by the crisis in the old-established coal industry in the Walloon areas with its socialist, anti-clerical and pro-French tradition, while agrarian Flanders has been gaining as a result of economic modernisation. Extreme Walloon and Flemish political parties complicate the division into three main camps – Christian-social, liberal and socialist. In Holland there is little resemblance between those who live in the polders by the sea and those who live in the softer rural areas of Maestricht. If you cross the frontier from France into Spain it is said that you step out of a country dominated by gardens into one which seems to belong to Africa rather than to Europe, where whatever is not mountain is either steppe or desert (that is, until you reach Seville or the British-haunted beaches). If you cross the frontier from France to Switzerland you move from a country that has known revolutions, invasions, defeats and victories into a country which is divided on linguistic and religious grounds but which, since the first cantons coming together in 1291 to Geneva at last joining the confederation in 1848, has concentrated upon establishing cooperation and peace. If you cross the frontier from France into Germany you find a country which is dramatically divided: into two German states, one of which is a federation; by the controversies about the tragedy and the guilt of the past; by the difficulty of identifying with the mean-looking provincial capital of Bonn; by the impossibility of ever again becoming an empire as well as a state; by the differences between north and south (Bismarck, the founder of the Second Reich, never forgot that he was insulted in the south because he refused to kneel down when a Catholic procession passed him, and Hitler, the founder of the Third Reich, visited Hamburg as rarely as possible); by the paradox of having become a great industrial state while remaining a forest people still surrounded by unbroken wooded slopes and still moved by the idea of Urwald, the primeval forest.

In the East the variety persists. One of the oldest nationalities, the Magyars of Hungary, lives in a land divided by mountains and by the rivers Danube and Tisza; they are haunted still by the number of Hungarians who live within other frontiers: Romania, Yugoslavia, Czechoslovakia. Finland, for long famous as the country of a thousand lakes, now claims other statistics: two million saunas for four million inhabitants; 95 per cent of the population are officially Lutheran, but only 5 per cent regularly practise their religion; the most northerly Islamic community in the world is Finnish, a small group of Moslem Tatars who took refuge there in the 1920s.

Contrasting northern and southern Europe from Helsinki to Palermo, contrasting rural and urban, considering the different ranges of Catholicism and Protestantism, reflecting on differences in manners, in styles of hospitality, in attitudes to food and dress, one can become bewildered by the concept of Europe. But no wonder American novelists have revelled in this diversity. In the lands and manners of Europe they have found endless material. Landscapes can change in what are to them very short distances, and over a range of mountains or the line of a river people change their ways of speaking or even their way of moving. Lionel Trilling admired the European novel because, among much else, 'it revelled in the hum and buzz of implication' which seemed dazzlingly dense to someone from a more open-textured society. No doubt this is why Henry James and others stayed in Europe.

Americans too are struck by the great variety which exists within each European city. Rarely laid out in rectangular blocks, European cities tell the story of long periods of development, of a series of historical stages, of change, reconstruction and experiment. In Prague, Budapest, Vienna, Frankfurt, Amsterdam, one can hardly turn a corner without coming across something startling, often a dramatic evocation of the city's past.

It is not surprising that, given this variety, European peoples attribute national characteristics to their neighbours. Sometimes it is the smell: the rain in England, the acrid cigarettes in France, the cheese in Holland, the outdoor cooking in Greece. Englishmen going to the continent are always struck by something in each country they visit: the careful taste with which rooms are furnished in Holland, the way they make the beds in Germany, the lateness of meals in Spain, the small satchel-carrying schoolchildren shaking hands with each other in France. From this it is easy to caricature one's neighbours, as the English caricature the Irish, the Scots, the Welsh, and particularly the French. The French, after all, still represent the immediate foreigner in English eyes; when English people travel to the Continent by car, they often pass through France even if that country is not their destination. So the dubious generalisations flourish, and since the French respond they clash: French formality and bureaucracy against English relaxed flexibility, English philistinism against French intellect and cultivation, French civilisation against the easier dispersed English style, English idealism against French national egoism, French commitment to Europe and to world policies against British insularity. Other countries make similar generalisations about their neighbours. Spaniards think, or pretend to think, that the Portuguese are slow-witted and a bit dull. Austrians tell the same sort of stories about the Germans, Poles about the Russians. Legends and myths about national characters abound: the French are said to be frivolous, the Irish beset by poetic fantasy, the Spaniards proud, the Greeks dishonest, the Poles heroic, the Swiss selfish. Sometimes these legends change, often to a country's advantage. Thus it was said that if you scratched a Frenchman, you would find a peasant

– thrifty, grasping, narrowminded, beset and bounded by the immediate horizon. But now the Frenchman is thought of as oversold on modernisation, gadgetry and change. It used to be said that Germany was both over-intellectual and bellicose. One German is a scholar, two Germans are a duet at the opera, three Germans are a war, French *lycéens* used to repeat in the days of the Third Republic. If a dying German is faced with two signs, one saying 'To Heaven' and the other saying 'To Lectures about Heaven', he will choose the latter, was the more kindly joke put about at the same time. But now the German is depicted as hard-working, practical, serious and totally devoted to increasing his material possessions, therefore peaceful. Sometimes the change in legend is to a country's disadvantage. Thus the Englishman was thought of as puritanical and industrious, with a strong sense of civic pride and discipline. Now the Englishman is more often considered to have a low sense of personal morality, to be lazy, self-centred and, as a worker, ready to go on strike at a moment's notice.

People create legends about themselves, usually pessimistic. Italians like to stress their failures. It has been said that while the British named a railway station after the great victory of Waterloo, if the Italians had to name a railway station after a battle they would name it Caporetto, after their defeat in the First World War. There are Frenchmen who claim that France is ungovernable, Englishmen who believe in the irreversible decline of England, Germans who say that Germany will never be forgiven for what they did in the war, Swedes who claim that the rest of the world is in a vast conspiracy of not acknowledging their achievements.

Where in all this is Europe, a conception of Europe, a sense of being European? A well-known Canadian journalist has told us that when he stepped on to Victoria Station in London at the age of seven, he knew he was in Europe. It smelled like Europe. The coal smoke from the railway engine, the porter's woodbine cigarette, the brown sugary tea in the station restaurant, the chill London fog that made the pavements glisten, all this for him was Europe. This is not because Victoria Station is like the Gare de l'Est in Paris, or like the great ornate station in Milan which so resembles a cathedral that people have been known to genuflect as they enter, but because English stood for European. At its best this meant liberty, tolerance, reason, respect for rights and a certain sense of human equality. It could be argued that these formalities were not present at the time of Hitler's Germany, Vichy France, Franco's Spain, Mussolini's Italy, the Colonels' Greece, Salazar's Portugal. But there was always Goethe's Germany and Weimar, Voltaire's France and the Republic, the Spain of Unamuno and Salvador de Madariaga, the liberal traditions of Italy and Greece. If England has become a more combative society over the last thirty years, if it has become more caught up in private and material gain, if the political consensus has increasingly disappeared, then this brings England closer to its continental neighbours and to current Western European practices and values.

Perhaps even within the facile generalisations which one nation makes about another there is, after all, an underlying sense of being European. If England and France are the most thin-skinned, the one towards the other, perhaps it is because the English feel that the French have a secret about how to live. It is something internal. It is not just the more obvious things, such as wine and cooking skills, or what is popularly believed to be their sophisticated attitude towards sexual matters. It is rather that once English people come to know France, even in very general and elementary terms, then they may become very attached to it. There is, in fact, an English disease which has been called French flu, whereby everything that is French is better than it is in England. The French do not always understand this. Why, asks a French sociologist, do the British not do things in the way they know best? The British are intuitively able to get the feel of a society, and the French can learn from them there. But the British insist upon whoring after French abstractions and theory-making.

In a similar way the French have a love-hate relationship with the Germans. It is impossible to forget the past when there is a memorial for the French dead in three Franco-German wars in every French town. But the French admire and envy what they see as the German virtues which have made them economically successful. When a French Prime Minister wishes to make a promise to his electorate he says, in 1987, that in five years time France will have overtaken Germany and will have become the leading economic power in Europe. Similarly, the Germans feel that it is the Italians who have an enviably frivolous style of living, succeeding apparently without serious effort. Other nations are envious of the strength of Polish Catholicism, the social commitment of the Scandinavian countries, the passionate attachment to folk music felt by the Magyars, the common sense of the Dutch. Many European countries admire the traditions of Great Britain, including Oxford and Cambridge, public schools and an atmosphere of deference.

What is important is that one European people should turn to another as an object of admiration. There has always been a time when certain European intellectuals have poured scorn upon European values. However, it is rare to find Europeans who admire the religious fundamentalism of Islam, the mysticism of Buddhism or Hinduism, the animism of Africa or, indeed, any of the political experiments or adventures in the Third World. European culture is therefore, whatever else it is, something which ultimately arouses the enthusiasm of Europeans.

But two problems now arise. One concerns Russia. Many Europeans have chosen the Russian Revolution of 1917 as a model which they wish to follow. For this and other reasons the question has to be asked: is Russia a part of Europe? The other problem concerns the United States. What is the role of this country in Europe, since many Europeans (and not only in Western Europe) identify themselves easily with the American way of life and assume that it is superior and desirable? One hundred and fifty years ago and more, acute observers such as the French liberal Alexis de Tocqueville predicted that these two nations were 'marked out by the will of Heaven to sway the destinies of half the globe'.

It is easy to point out how Russian history is different from that of other European states. Russian Christianity was cut off from the Europe where papal power was developing. Russia underwent no Renaissance, no Reformation, no Counter-Reformation; there was no check to central government from Churches, middle classes, regional loyalties, the aristocracy; there was always a vast gulf between the government and the people and, in spite of the Revolution of 1917 and its evolution, some would maintain that there still is. But this does not mean that because of this and because in the nineteenth century Russia colonised vast Asian lands, Russia should be thought of as a Euro-Asian state. Russia is part of the European system and many European values are accepted in Russia. But Russia is such a special case, and of such extension and power, that it cannot easily be considered at the same time as other states whose history is more directly interwoven with that of Western and Central Europe.

As for the United States most European observers, from the eighteenth century onwards, appreciated its expansion, its demographic and commercial growth, and its invulnerability from attack. As travel became easier it was possible for Britons and Americans to discover how much they had in common (and how easy it was for the great political families of England, the Chamberlains, Churchills and Harcourts, to make American marriages). But other countries have found it more difficult. French and German farmers at the end of the nineteenth century found themselves threatened by the agricultural surpluses of the Midwest. Aristocratic Europe resented the republican, money-grabbing, hustling life which America represented. Between the wars American debt policy created animosity and in some continental countries America was regarded as a non-culture, an unfortunate racial mix that was bound to be ineffective. After 1945 there were many in Europe who resented American wealth, and who were frightened that American interference in European politics and apparent devotion to the Cold War could bring about further disasters. Now, since within the United States the Atlanticist east coast is losing out to the different elements of the West and the South, there is a new fear that the United States will abandon a Europe which its leaders do not respect and which its population admires only in cosy tourist terms. It is curious that there was, diplomatically and strategically, a movement for European countries to unite in order to reduce American influence, while now one can see a movement for European countries to unite more firmly because there is fear of an American pull-out.

In some respects the United States can be seen as a transplant of Europe and European consciousness. In other respects, not. The gap – social, cultural and political – widens all the time. Much of this is cultural. Socialism, so important in Europe, has scarcely touched America. Religious fundamentalism, so important in America, has little echo in Europe. American extremism, whether in nationalism or in cultural power, offends the moderation which Europeans traditionally venerate. If *Dallas* and *Dynasty* play an important part in the lives of the whole of Western Europe, they present a world of ostentatious wealth, power and violence which is far distant from the world of European soap operas. No wonder that in 1986 European public service broadcasters met in Vienna to try and devise means of combating this American cultural imperialism. No wonder that no one believes they have the slightest chance of success.

But within the diversity of the continent we have to take account of how different European states view both Russia and America. The European diversity is increased by the obligation of having to take sides, pro-Soviet or pro-American. But the diversity is even greater. In France, for example, there is a longstanding fear of American culture taking over French culture, and the government officially bans the use of English words (you must not say 'marketing' but 'mercantique', you must not pay 'cash' but 'comptant', and 'le knowhow' is replaced by 'le savoir-faire'). This susceptibility is far from being shared by the West Germans who revel in the use of English-American expressions (is this because the language which the Germans have sent abroad is largely the language of war, words such as 'blitzkrieg', 'U-boat', 'howitzer'?). Yet it was French intellectuals who first explained to the world that Hollywood films were not simply entertainment but productions of profound significance. French drugstores represent a fascinating cross-breeding of French and American influences. It is in France, not in West Germany, that an enormous Disneyland park is to be created. And, in a similar paradox, though the French have always claimed a special relationship with the Russians as one revolutionary country to another, it is in France that the revulsion against the Soviet gulag has been most explicitly elucidated.

Both America and Russia participate in what can be thought of as European culture, both traditional and experimental, in music, opera, ballet, theatre. But it is in the novel, above all else, that Europe has explored its main preoccupations: the interrelations of the individual, class, marriage, the family, personal relationships, money, property, power, religion. There is a line of growth which runs across Europe from Russia to England, and which encompasses America. Imaginatively, the novel is the greatest of European inventions and achievements, the best key to understanding Europe in all its differences and all its forms of unity. East Europeans frequently remind us that Dickens and Balzac belong to them as much as they do to us, and we do not need reminding that Dostoevsky and Tolstoy are an essential part of our tradition.

In a more purely intellectual area, there is the European tradition of social analysis. You cannot begin the study of society without drawing on the great names: Mill, Tocqueville, Beccaria, Marx, Durkheim, Weber, Pareto. This Europe of the mind is part of a critical tradition, analytical, sceptical, probing. It befits a continent where the belief in freedom of speech has appeared and re-appeared so frequently as to be a constant. In this century that discipline has been hugely furthered by America. By now America must have more social scientists than all other countries put together.

We must not forget another pan-European element, which is the Jew. From earliest times most of the states of Europe had Jewish minorities who lived at the whim of their rulers. Where the minority was small the Jews were usually town dwellers and had little to do with farming. They could not join the guilds (which controlled entry to the different craft professions) because these were Christian fraternities, and the Jews' religious obligation not to work on the Sabbath restricted their activities. They therefore became even more inward-looking, a group determined to survive by binding themselves together with laws and rituals. Perhaps too, many Jews became moneylenders because their highest ideal was to study the Torah, Jewish law and religion; an occupation such as moneylending permitted long hours of study and piety. But in areas where larger Jewish communities existed, as in the Mediterranean countries and in eastern Europe from later medieval times, the Jewish occupations were more diverse. They became artisans and traders, often turning to occupations which others did not want to touch. From early times they were a diverse population. Jews were given freedom first of all in Britain and in Holland, but in the late eighteenth century, under a series of decrees, the Jews of Russia (including Russian Poland) were confined to a specified area or part of the country. Conditions of poverty were worsened after 1881 by pogroms and by a period of repression. Consequently some two million Jews left Russia and areas of Poland which were ruled by Germany and Austria and travelled westward, many of them aiming for America.

One must emphasise the diversity of these populations and the difficulties in their relations with those Jewish communities in England, France, Holland and elsewhere, who had largely become assimilated to their national groups. But although in most countries there were protestations about the immigration and anti-Semitism increased, they took their place successfully. It was noted in London, for example, that the increase of the Jewish population in Whitechapel led to an increase in the respectability of the area.

The story of Jews in Western Europe is usually associated with success. Whether we are thinking of innumerable small businesses or artisan enterprises, or such magnates as Montagu Burton of Leeds, the Jews can be described as acting like the yeast within more solid bodies. But the stories of success are never stories of unspecified success. If Burton opened more than 500 retail shops before 1939 (in competition with the non-Jewish Fifty Shilling Tailors) the post-war transition to more informal menswear led to the closure of his factories in the 1970s.

The history of European Jewry makes nonsense of European frontiers and stereotypes. The son of a rabbi tells how his mother gave birth to the members of her large family in different capitals, as she moved from east to west; one, for example, in Budapest, then another in the railway station at Milan. We also know the story of an Italian Jewish family whose ancestors sold rags in the ghetto near Turin. The revolutions of 1848 and the unification of Italy gave them civic equality and the chance to emerge. They became distinguished by their patriotism and their wealth. Some joined the fascist party and became influential supporters of Mussolini. (As semi-observant Jews they made astonishing mistakes; one woman knew so little Hebrew that each day she recited a prayer which thanked God for making her a man.) The anti-Jewish laws caught them by surprise, but their versatility persisted. The young man of the family emigrated to Palestine, worked on a kibbutz, joined the British army and eventually became a professor.

It was in the middle of the nineteenth century that international finance assumed a new importance in Europe. Jewish firms were prominent in this, such as the Rothschilds (the five sons of Mayer Amschel Rothschild had settled in Frankfurt, London, Paris, Vienna and Naples), Erlanger (from Frankfurt), Grant (originally from Dublin), Lazard Brothers (from Paris). It has been argued that the operations of these financiers depended upon confidence and trust and that this was often best established by means of a shared origin and faith. But this was not confined to the Jewish community; it existed among Protestant bankers and financiers as well as among Greeks, and there are examples of banks that were ostentatiously Catholic (as there are of families that moved out of the Jewish community, such as the Oppenheims).

Perhaps the lesson that one should draw from the role of the Jews in Europe is that Europe is not merely diverse and international. Europe is essentially cosmopolitan.

Yet within the variety there exists a unity. Landscapes may differ greatly, but they also have common qualities which if viewed from, say, Asia make them recognisably European. There are no great deserts, and there is only one sizeable mountain range. Climates are generally temperate, and they are often described in a very European phrase – liveable-in. Landscapes are usually manageable, man-manageable, fit for humans to live in. E. M. Forster in *A Passage to India* writes about the inhumanity and the alienness of that part of the Indian subcontinent which is near his Marabar caves. This is not the sort of landscape which will encourage you to create a religion presided over by a loving God, a God who cares for each individual and who is to be found in the woods and streams and lanes, he writes. It suggests rather a God without feeling for the little human beings who try to make a life in that hostile, uncaring setting; not at all the God you imagine in England's cosy Lake District or South Downs, in the Black Forest or in Burgundy. Kipling, also writing about India, has a story about a man who proposes to the wrong girl in a dust storm. How can one have love in a landscape where that sort of thing is possible?

Europe is particularly privileged with regard to communications. No other continent has so dense a network. There are the great rivers, such as the Danube which flows for 2800 miles through half a dozen nation-states, past three capitals and many other cities. Victor Hugo, finishing a book on the Rhine in 1841, remarked that this river brought together two countries which were the twin keystones of Europe: Germany, which was northern and eastern, leaned on the Baltic, the Adriatic and the Black Sea, and used as flying-buttresses Sweden, Denmark, Greece and the Danubian principalities; France, which was southern and western, leaned on the Mediterranean and the Atlantic, and used Italy and Spain as supports. The Rhine, according to Hugo, linked Germany, the Europe which felt, the Europe which had a heart, and France, the Europe which thought, the Europe which had a brain.

Then there are the canals, the roads, the railways, the air network, all the man-made means of communication which have been made to satisfy the needs of trade, industrialisation, war and curiosity. More motorways are being built. We in Europe take it for granted that this intricate overlapping and often duplicating pattern of ways of getting around and physically communicating will be there. But if one tries to travel from an African state to a neighbouring African state one finds enormous difficulties. Since the colonisers made the communications run to their own capitals, especially London and Paris, it is still sometimes necessary to travel from one part of West Africa to another via Europe.

There are other means of easy communication in Europe. A plastic bank card will be accepted in most places. There is direct dialling. There are shared television programmes and satellites. There are more or less agreed assumptions about timekeeping and the working day. The same kinds of conveyor belt and computer rattle all over Europe, and a similar work ethic can sometimes bring the same conflicts between industrialists and their 'hands' (as they used to call them) in every country. This is nothing new. There have always been factories all over Europe making the same things, often in the same way. In the 1930s there were two countries in Western Europe which made 'shoddy', a cheap reconstituted cloth which made millions of bluey-grey blankets for the British and German armies. They were at Dewsbury, some eight miles out of Leeds, and at Wuppertal, in the Ruhr, both small towns. There have always been trade unionists – from northern Italy, northern

France, northern Germany — who faced the same problems and who spoke the same language.

International companies, banks, stock exchanges, currency dealers, all unite Europe. (A millionaire French communist, recently deceased, used to bring Eastern and Western Europe together in deals over agrarian products.) They are now more important than the royal families and the aristocracy which used to intermarry. More important too perhaps is that odd invention, the man's two-piece or three-piece suit and European formal morning dress. Everywhere in Europe one can see the unifying influence of woman's fashions, whether from the great dress designers or the ready-mades. Orchestras move from one European town to another. Exhibitions and theatrical companies travel easily. Film buffs in London or Prague know what is happening in Spain or Sweden. It can be argued that all this will mean that a pan-European consumer society will be produced. But it also means that a European is never alone. Everywhere he is at home.

The Gloriette, Schönbrunn, Vienna 'The greatest monarch on the proudest throne is obliged to sit upon his own arse' (Benjamin Franklin)

4 · PYRAMIDS AND PLAINS

All societies are unequal. Tribal bands develop into states through the gradual accumulation of power in the hands of a chief and his entourage. A thousand years before Christ, Hindu society became divided into castes. Some five hundred years later the Chinese gave power to those who could pass competitive examinations. The Aztecs had a most rigidly enforced system of class distinctions, and a man could be executed if he were discovered to be wearing the insignia of a class superior to his own.

But the idea and the practice of hierarchy is essentially European. No other continent, including those which have been peopled mainly by Europeans, has such a selfconscious, determined, labelled and discussed sense of inequality. The history of Europe is the history of 'them' and 'us'. This means the awareness of authority, which comes to every child as he or she sees a complex society in which the rent collector, the school attendance officer, the policeman, play their roles; and which comes to every adult as he or she makes the acquaintance of the tax collector, the conscription officer, the manager, the trade union representative, the police, the local authority. And further, there are the institutions; the state, the Church, the political party, the army. This is the inequality of power – on one hand, those who have authority; on the other, those who have to accept that authority. But there is also the inequality of class, which depends upon money – where you are placed in terms of your productive capacity, or of your ownership (or not) of the means of production. There is, too, the inequality of status, which is concerned with prestige, with social estimation, with style of living and means of consumption. All three are extremely complex, and all three can be confused. Because Europe is an old continent and because its societies become increasingly complicated and sophisticated, it is no wonder that these inequalities have become preoccupations.

This is all the more so because in Europe these inequalities have been, and are, most frequently denounced, and measures have been taken to abolish or change them. There has always been a myth, prevalent among most European peoples, that there was once a happy age when primitive men and women lived contentedly together in a state of equality, before there were lords and masters, rich and poor. This golden age might have existed before the Fall of Man, it might have represented an Arcadia, it might have been the period of the noble savage, it could have existed in Homeric Greece, in Anglo-Saxon England before the Norman invasion, in Celtic France before the Franks, on the great Danubian plain before the Magyars. The discovery of America, and travellers' tales like the later discoveries in the Pacific Islands, periodically encouraged beliefs in an early paradise where a simple equality reigned. In England the peasant rebels in 1381 asked

> 'When Adam delved and Eve span
> Who then was the gentleman?'

Montaigne in the sixteenth century suggested that it was the use of metals, improvements in agriculture and the rise of the arts and sciences which had brought about the end of communal ownership and led to the differentiation between rich and poor and to economic and political subjection. During the English Civil War

Thomas Rainborowe, in October 1647, uttered the famous words, 'The poorest he that is in England has a life to live as the greatest he.' Rainborowe is here the spokesman for democracy, which always implied that there should be a substantial degree of equality among men. Rousseau distinguished two types of inequality, the natural, which arose from considerations of age, health and mind, and that which was the result of a convention. During the French Revolution it was Gracchus Babeuf who most clearly put forward the principle that men should not only be given equality before the law but should be treated equally in terms of their rewards and their needs.

Demands for equality went hand in hand with great hostility to the institutions of kingship and the aristocracy, the most longstanding instances of inequality. The role of kings and princes is determined by a mixture of considerations, sometimes prowess in war, sometimes magical powers, sometimes by holding the balance between warring factions within the state, sometimes by policies of marriage and inheritance. But by the end of medieval times rulers, in the forms of monarchs, asserted their military strength over their too-powerful subjects and extended their administrative powers so as to unify their states. This is what happened in England, France, Spain, Portugal, Sweden, and later in Russia. In the smaller states within Germany and Italy this pattern was also followed. This meant that the state became identified with a ruler, or a ruling family. Royal or princely families depended upon succession by means of blood ties, and what counted was not the functioning of the institution, nor the quality of the ruler, but the identity of the ruler. You did not say to royalty, 'What have you accomplished?' You asked who royalty was, from whom they were descended.

Thus there grew up in Europe a great trade-unionism of monarchies and royal families. Each king, or prince, was expected to hold a court and in that court he was expected to show himself as being grander than other mortals. The ritual of court life, all the ceremony surrounding royal births, marriages, deaths, the pageantry of receptions and royal pastimes, the distribution of honours, all these were meant to demonstrate that the ruler was not like other men, but possessed magical and mystical powers. It was by divine will that the rulers were there (and as late as the beginning of the eighteenth century, there were those in England who believed in the royal touch, that Queen Anne could cure ailments). The court could also be used as a tactical device. Powerful nobles could be lured or attracted into taking up positions in court and would thereby lose their power to act as a force hostile to the monarch.

The court of Louis XIV of France became the model for all others. Every ruler in Europe who could do so built a palace like Versailles, and imitated the elaborate French court ritual. This was the period of absolutism, when theoretically the power of the king began nowhere and ended nowhere because it was everywhere. But this did not mean that monarchs were 'absolute' in the sense that they could do anything. It was generally agreed in seventeenth-century Europe that there were only two rulers, both considered to be outside Europe, who had this sort of power – the rulers of the Ottoman Empire and of Russia. And when in 1654 the Tsar of Russia rode out of Moscow to make war on Poland, the young Tsar Alexis, magnificent as any Bourbon with the hooves of his horse set with pearls and his personal standard sewn with gold, marked Russia's re-emergence as a European power.

The royal families of Europe made war against each other. But they also intermarried. The families of small states were often in demand as royal consorts because they were 'of the royal blood'. From the Gonzaga family, which ruled over Mantua for some five centuries, came Luisa, queen to two successive kings of Poland in the seventeenth century, and her sister Anna, who became the Princess Palatine and was much celebrated in France. In the nineteenth century the house of Saxe-Coburg-Gotha, a small German state, furnished Queen Victoria's mother and then her consort, Prince Albert; the husband to the Queen of Portugal; the husband to the Princess of Orleans of France; the wife of her brother, the Duke of Nemours; and the King of Belgium after 1830.

Royalty was surrounded by deference and affection. Queen Victoria had known what it was to be booed in the streets, but her death was felt as a personal loss throughout the United Kingdom. The shopkeepers of Vienna would stand outside their shops every morning to bow to the Emperor Francis Joseph as he rode by. Loyalty in Germany to the Emperor William II was fanatical. Yet the monarchies did not survive the wars. The prophecy attributed to King Farouk of Egypt, that there would soon be only five kings left, the King of England and the four kings of a pack of cards, has not quite come about (although there is no longer a king of Egypt). But monarchies now exist only in the Scandinavian countries, in Holland, Belgium and Great Britain, and in smaller states such as Luxembourg and Monaco. These Western institutions make a conscious effort to be democratic and their ceremonial has been transformed, notably because of television cameras. But the most significant revival of monarchy has been in Spain, where the transition from dictatorship to parliamentary monarchy has been carried out under the aegis of King Juan Carlos. In all monarchies, but especially in Spain, the emphasis now is less on the mystique and more on the usefulness. One is reminded of the old saying, 'A king is a thing men have made for their own sakes, for quietness' sake, just as in a family one man is appointed to buy meat.'

Yet the existence of monarchies had been central to the organisation of European society, at the top of a great hierarchy in which everyone was included. All living creatures were part of what was sometimes called 'the great chain of being' and everyone had his place in the order, which was regarded as natural and conferred by birth. But in a continent like Europe, where there was constant economic change, there was also constant pressure to modify this ladder of rank. Sometimes this was expressed by a small change in habits. In the seventeenth century, when the Quakers refused to remove their hats in the presence of their superiors because they believed in the equality of man, they were regarded as dangerous; in eighteenth-century England it became common not to doff one's hat to a social superior. This was partly because the London streets were becoming crowded and it was not easy to recognise who was who. In seventeenth-century France there was much discussion of the definition of social groups and there was much squabbling among the members of the different 'estates' into which French society was divided; often processions and ceremonies were delayed because the participants, possibly members of some municipal authority, could not agree on their order of precedence. In central Europe reforms abolished certain conditions of serfdom.

But the key to changes in society probably comes from changes in vocabulary. Words like 'rank', 'degree', 'station', 'order' or 'interest' gradually gave way to the word, and to the concept of, 'class'. This did not only apply to England, where a dictionary defined 'class' as 'an order, or distribution of people' as early as 1656, but to France where 'les classes' came to replace 'les états' and to Germany where 'die Schichten' became 'die Klasse'. Soon people were talking about three different sorts of classes, 'landlords, capitalists and labourers', and in the course of the nineteenth century many refinements were added. But there were two easy simplifications: one was to ignore these distinctions in favour of the simple contrast between rich and poor, Babeuf's 'gilded bellies' and 'empty bellies', Disraeli's 'two nations'. The other to assert class solidarity, especially in the middle classes and later, in 'the industrious', or 'the working classes' as they came to be known.

This class solidarity became one of the great cementing features in European life. The ideas and assumptions that bind a society together have had to do with the social class and its sense of itself, its sense of fitting in, its conception of duties, its idea of what are its dues. From this there grew two other cementing ideas: the concern with material welfare, with property and the handing on of property; and the concern with marriage and the family. It is no accident that the European novel enshrined the complex meanings of those concepts, their elaborate dance through time and space. Jane Austen, Dickens, Balzac, Galdos, Thomas Mann and Mauriac all wrote novels about property, money, status, marriage and the ways in which individuals can fit in with the values and standards of their societies.

It is hardly surprising that it was the middle class which attracted most solidarity and praise, mainly from the emergent, educated and vocal middle class itself. The very conception of a middle class seemed to be fortunate: it suggested an avoidance of extremes, a centrality and harmony within the social system, a golden mean or *juste-milieu*. It was necessary to have a class of men who were educated, who had adequate time at their disposal and who were (theoretically at least) not attached to any built-in system of privilege if the affairs of the state and the community were to be attended to. Little wonder that Lord Brougham described the middle classes as the wealth and intelligence of the country and 'the glory of the British name', that Guizot saw the ascendancy of the middle classes as the natural destiny of French history, that countless Italian and German businessmen, together with lawyers and teachers, believed that they should dominate the political life of their countries.

With class pride and solidarity go class attitudes. There is the story of a question which was set in a school scholarship examination: 'You notice the doctor, then a lawyer, then a policeman going quickly into a house near your home. Explain what is happening.' One child answers that the well-to-do widow living there has been found dead, without warning; the doctor is called by the housekeeper and he thinks that she must have had a massive stroke, but just to be on the safe side he calls a policeman; the dead woman's son is telephoned at work and he immediately sets off for the house, but not before telephoning the family solicitor to meet him at once, since there's a will to be read. But another child, who lives in a poorer district, explains that there has been a drunken punch-up in the house; the doctor is called and he immediately sends for the police as he realises that charges will be made; the man who's done the beating-up knows his rights and demands a lawyer. Further examples could be given, each one using finer and finer subdivisions of class. When questions are heavy with possible cultural meanings then they will have several 'right' answers.

W. H. Auden had a fine eye for the nuances of society. In a private letter he described himself as coming from the professional middle class, and being proud of it. He believed in doing a fair day's work and being paid fairly for it. He would pay his own debts off at once and could not bear to buy anything on hire-purchase. He saw himself and his kind as the sustaining seam of society, that which more than any other made society work. But while they were at their posts, the upper classes, who owed money to the middle classes for goods and services and who paid only when they felt like it, went off to the races. There they were joined by the working classes who had failed to turn up for work at the middle-class person's establishment, having falsely claimed sickness so that they could draw benefit money.

A man whom Auden particularly admired was Walter Scott,

whom he described as 'a bourgeois saint'. Quite late in life Scott found himself and his family threatened by bankruptcy. He could not stand the shame of this, in spite of the fact that a declaration of bankruptcy would presumably have meant payment of only a small amount in the pound to the creditors. Therefore he began writing furiously in order to pay off his debts, £114,000, in full. This is a Scottish story, a British story, an essential European story.

Of course there is an element of caricature in these views. As we can see in Scandinavia, in Britain or in the Low Countries, the middle classes adapt very well to the existence of royal families and they show little independence when it comes to receiving royal honours. In those countries which do not have monarchies and where there is freedom of expression, magazine and newspaper accounts of royal families are favourite reading for the middle classes. But the monarchical principle, that of the blood royal, has gone. Few who proclaim their loyalty would consider that the rightful monarch of England is an obscure Bavarian prince, or that the rightful claimant to the throne of France is Alphonse, Duke of Anjou and Cadiz. Monarchies are matters of convenience or entertainment.

More puzzling is the persistence of the aristocracy. The British aristocracy has survived and can be said to have reconstituted itself, after the erosion caused by taxation and land sales, as an upper class. Indeed if, as some believe, England as a whole is becoming something of a museum piece, then the British aristocracy, with its country houses, art collections, style and manners is becoming a valuable asset. But the aristocracies of Western Europe are still evident, with their titles, their castles, their gracious living and their wealth. Most surprising of all, the French aristocracy, supposedly both disinherited and decapitated by the French Revolution, still exists and flourishes. Many families continue to live in the châteaux where their ancestors lived before 1789; the *Bottin Mondain* is more commonly found in France than *Burke's Peerage* is in Britain; a glance at the names of those who serve in the Corps Diplomatique shows the role which the aristocracy still plays in state affairs. The story is told of a French aristocratic family in the 1890s who discovered that one of their servants had purloined a piece of silver. They constituted a court of justice along the lines of seignorial jurisdiction, and found the servant guilty. He was then taken out to the neighbouring woods and hanged; the local police were told that he had been caught in the act of stealing and had committed suicide. The anecdote, whether true or false, suggests that it is easy to believe that the power and sense of privilege of an aristocratic family could persist more than a century after the storming of the Bastille.

There are several reasons for the ways in which the European aristocracy has been able to maintain its position. There is the obvious one, that the landed aristocracy were never exclusively landed, but took part in the industrial and commercial processes in spite of legends that they were too superior to dirty their hands. Another is the development, in most European countries, of a need for manifestations of the past which is more than the entertainment of nostalgia. Thus the aristocracy, in addition to being property developers and directors of multi-nationals, are involved in the national heritage business or *patrimoine* as the French call it. But perhaps the most potent reason is that in spite of the challenges to the aristocracy made by the bourgeoisie, clocked up in the French Revolution, or the 1832 Reform Act in England, or the Frankfurt Parliament which emerged from the 1848 revolutions in Germany, the most ambitious and the richest of the middle classes found much to admire in aristocratic values, manners and style. In the long run they sought to emulate and to join the aristocracy. We have to assimilate the concept of the aristocratic bourgeoisie. We have to record the fact that in Europe no revolution is ever complete, no revolution ever sweeps the board.

If for centuries, throughout Europe, the energies and actions of several layers of society were fuelled by considerations of class, property, money in stocks and shares, marriage settlements, family interests and inheritance, one has to ask whether these considerations applied universally, and whether or not they existed in the consciousness of common people. To some extent they did. In peasant societies there was an intense concern for the future – what would happen to the land, what would be the conditions of tenancy, who would inherit. There was always a danger of change. A government would alter its tariff laws and cheap wheat would be imported. A new railway would carry cattle or agricultural products to the local market. A different landlord or a recently arrived neighbour would start a programme of improvements. But such peasant attitudes were necessarily localised. However much a peasant from Tuscany or Bavaria resembled a peasant from Normandy or Castile, their preoccupations were not part of the interlocking, class–property–family thrust which held European society together and which gave it a peculiar driving force; those were bourgeois and upper-class preoccupations.

There was always a class which had no property, which lived in rented houses, which possessed no stocks and shares, which never made a will. Inheritance went usually by word of mouth, so that a particular person could claim that he or she had been destined to receive a silver sugar bowl or a set of knives and forks. In the 1930s there were families in Germany who discovered that their ancestors had been Jewish. Only then did they understand certain ornaments which had been casually passed on to them.

When the Italian statesman Cavour visited England in 1835 he commented, 'The English know how to work together; they know how to discuss without altercation and to respect individual opinions,' but he was talking only about the middle class, the class that he admired. Lower classes were not involved in working or discussing together. The French talk about 'l'esprit du clocher', the mental horizon bounded by one's village church spire. Max Weber professed to admire farmworkers rather than their aristocratic, or *Junker*, landlords, but what he praised in them was their sense of personal responsibility, a basic drive towards higher things, their physical and emotional qualities, all things which were individual. The middle to upper classes were involved in the process and the thrust of European life; they were active agents in the drama. But those who were in a lower social class were only brought on stage to swell a scene or two.

Usually that stage was war. In 1915 Italian peasants were mobilised and sent north to fight against the Austrians. Whether because they understood little about the reasons for the war and little attempt was made to explain things to them, or because they were poorly equipped and badly led, the battle of Caporetto was disastrous. But when this was followed by the threat of an Austrian invasion, the country as a whole seemed to rally. French peasants too were taken away from their farms and sent to the trenches to suffer appalling losses. They probably understood little about the causes of the war, in 1914 or in 1939, and their main thoughts were probably about the harvest. But the education which they had received after the laws of the 1880s had taught them patriotism, and their letters home showed that they identified with the national cause. Perhaps it was most difficult for the English working class, who had to go to faraway countries, only leaving their island in order to fight for it. Thomas Hardy writes about Drummer Hodge, killed in the Boer War and buried on the veldt:

> Yet portion of that unknown plain
> Will Hodge for ever be;
> His homely Northern breast and brain
> Grow to some Southern tree,
> And strange-eyed constellations reign
> His stars eternally.

The extraordinary thing was that when men were transported from their fields or their factory benches to the battlefields, they found in the army a sense of cohesion, fellowship and social endeavour which they had not found at home. They found too that governments showed an interest in their welfare which had been missing before.

If the aristocracy is liable to fall victim to the sin of pride, if the working classes are liable to succumb to the defeats of deference, the middle class tends to cupidity. The essence of most bourgeois societies was profit, and the assumption that it is right and proper for a minority of the community to live at the expense of the majority. It is appropriate that a character in one of Balzac's novels should have said that it was not King Louis Philippe who reigned over France but the golden sovereign, the *louis d'or*. The phrase 'One half of the world doesn't know how the other half lives' is said to date from 1725.

But when industrialisation came it seemed that equality was a possibility. If a man, working at a machine, could produce more goods in a few days than he himself would ever require, then there was no reason why anyone should lack these goods. It was simply a matter of distribution. Some writers thought it inevitable that a great equality would come about and that the proletariat (whether referred to by this term or not) would advance towards a greater equality with the social classes above it. John Stuart Mill, in 1830, recalled that eight centuries earlier society was divided into barons and serfs, but not a century had gone by which had not lowered the powerful and raised the low. Marx believed that the gap between the bourgeoisie and the proletariat was getting wider, but he believed that the remedy was at hand. 'Workers of the world unite; cast off your chains; the day of redemption is at hand.' Tocqueville believed that political democracy inevitably went hand in hand with a desire for equality. 'Democratic communities,' he wrote, 'have a natural taste for freedom; left to themselves they will seek it, cherish it, and view any privation with regret. But for equality their passion is ardent, insatiable, incessant, invincible; they call for equality in freedom and if they cannot obtain that they call for equality in slavery. They will endure poverty, servitude, barbarism, slavery, but they cannot endure aristocracy.'

By Tocqueville's 'aristocracy' we should read all forms of assumed social superiority. Jane Austen's Emma, having visited a sick cottager, says, 'I feel now as if I could think of nothing but these poor creatures all the rest of the day; and yet who can say how soon it may all vanish from my mind?' It can be argued that such attitudes have passed. It was some years ago that the French writer George Simenon heard a woman ordering fish in a shop and saying that one lot need not be fresh because it was 'for the servants'. Some years ago too it was that a middle-class woman in an expensive grocer's shop in Harrogate gave an order for delivery ending with 'and a pound of maid's bacon'. It can be argued that you are not likely to hear such remarks anywhere in Europe today.

It has always been said that class distinctions are associated with capitalism, and since the economic development of Europe was dominated by the play of capital, this would explain why Europe has been so distinguished by consciousness of class. The concentration of capital in a few hands placed capitalists and their families at the top of the social ladder. The leader of Germany in the early 1920s, Dr Rathenau, claimed that the economic life of Europe was controlled by some three hundred individuals, and it used to be said that when Lord Melchett smiled there was sunshine in ten thousand homes. It can therefore be argued that since, in most parts of Europe, capitalism has been modified by state action and by the effectiveness of trade union movements, class distinctions should have been modified as well. Further, since certain parts of Central and Eastern Europe have become communist, and Karl Marx after all looked to a classless society, social classes in these countries must have been abolished altogether.

To some extent this is true. The English historian R. H. Tawney, who gave a celebrated series of lectures on equality in 1929, liked to say that the English miners, who went into battle at Passchendaele and at the Somme, did not own property to the value of the kit which they took with them. Today, throughout Western Europe the harsher forms of class distinction – based upon money and wealth, and the power that they confer – have been modified. Working men, manual labourers, have become property owners. Thanks to action by the state or local authorities, there is social equality in terms of roads, lighting, water supply, minimum education, medical attendance, police protection, and a whole variety of benefits which are now secured irrespective of individual economic resources, but which were once dependent upon the ability of people to pay for them.

In a communist country such as East Germany, one can claim that equality has been attained. There is not a wide gulf between different economic situations; most people receive roughly similar wages, and differentials are modest. People tend to dress alike and to eat the same subsidised food.

But in both Western and Eastern Europe we have to recognise that class distinctions persist, and are not based upon simple economic contrasts. It is not a question of haves and have-nots. It is a question of status, relative positions on hierarchical ladders varying from country to country, from time to time. It does not matter whether or not you are a worker gaining an impressive wage, and able to own your own home, your car, your luxuries. What matters is whether or not you get your hands dirty, whether or not you have the correct accent or ease of speaking. Someone in a clerical job may well feel that he is superior, even if his income is less than that of a manual worker. Whatever the income level, in a country such as England many powerful vestiges of traditional assumptions and attitudes remain. Certain classes have an easy assumption of superiority which is confirmed when they see that those who have been to public school predominate in Oxford and Cambridge and those who have been to Oxford or Cambridge predominate in gaining places in the higher administrative branches of the Civil Service and in other important professions.

But it is most rewarding to examine a country such as Germany. One would expect both Germanies to have made a break with the past. The Nazi experience, the havoc caused by the war, and the communist takeover of the East constitute real revolutions. Germany had to start from scratch, and in the 1950s West Germany was often compared to America in its early days. One comparison was to say that West Germany was a classless society where prosperity was shared. You could go into a restaurant and be certain that workers and management were present and it would be difficult to tell which were which. There was no Oxford or Cambridge, no schools which had a particular snob value, no *grandes écoles* system as in France where elites are formed by their ability to pass competitive examinations. Furthermore, the German working class never built up its own culture as happened in England, and therefore had no inhibitions about adopting new ways of living and working.

Yet observers have recently noted that there are class differences. A worker, when he leaves his factory, tends to dress rather formally, even (it is said) if he is only going shopping with his wife. Management or intellectuals or members of the liberal professions will usually dress casually. The worker likes to take his holidays gregariously, and spends time in bars, swimming pools and on beaches. It is thought superior to go in for relative isolation when relaxing, and to go for walks in the forest or in the mountains. Workers are acquisitive. As money comes in they spend it on furniture, gadgets, a new car, home decoration. The higher social strata ostentatiously avoid this. Most striking of all is the reluctance of many worker families to encourage their children to have higher education, even when they can afford it and when the children have ability. It is as if there is a relic of the idea that people should know their place. It is significant too that, in spite of all the upheavals, in West Germany the aristocracy still flourishes.

In East Germany, as in other communist countries, the senior officials of the party enjoy many privileges, although this appears to be less marked than elsewhere. Sporting heroes are well treated and entertainers are affluent. But even in this officially classless society, which is by its very nature non-competitive, it has been noted that people tend to form small groups of twenty or thirty. Essentially these are people who feel at ease with each other. They often contain a mixture of professions and they are not necessarily political. It is as if a group society is being formed to make up for the absence of classes, with people seeking what they consider to be their own social levels.

This will not come as a surprise to those who criticised Marx for his failure to envisage the possibility that in a socialist society a new ruling class and new social distinctions would emerge. Indeed it has been argued that all societies which are communist are necessarily elite societies, where a small number of people take decisions concerning the economy or the provision of services, without any independent intermediary bodies to control them. There is the great mass of the population on one hand, and the management elite, a superior and powerful class, on the other.

Ought one then to agree with George Orwell who once remarked, 'No advance in wealth, no softening of manners, no reform or revolution has ever brought human equality a millimeter nearer'?

It could be argued that Orwell was writing within a clear European tradition, whereby the belief in the desirability of equality and the need for equality were accepted, and one talked about the French Revolution, the 1848 revolutions, socialism and Marxism as if they were to be taken for granted. It is as if the word 'equality' was used without too much discussion about its implications. There is, however, a more American view of equality which is based upon the principle of equality of opportunity. This is sometimes called 'non-egalitarian classlessness'. It is said that everyone, irrespective of his or her origins, has the same chance of reaching the highest levels in the occupational system. Each man, supposedly, is master of his own fate, and each man's destiny is determined by merit and circumstances (probably with the hope of a bit of luck).

This American view of equality has doubtless become more easily acceptable because it implies a certain conservatism. The existing social order can be maintained along with equality of opportunity. You do not need to assume an antagonism between classes; on the contrary, you can assume a readiness among the superior strata to accept a certain amount of social mobility. It is all the more acceptable because while this social mobility is a subject about which the European nations can be proud, pointing to Prime Ministers with humble social origins or to other important figures who have made their way by effort and ability, in fact the amount of movement from bottom to top is limited and hardly disturbs the acceptable face of existing society. Equality of opportunity is in no way incompatible with the nature of capitalist society. The move from rags to riches occurs and is appreciated, but it is rare.

Since diversity is one of the characteristics of Europe, it would be surprising if, in spite of the long tradition in favour of equality, this equality were applauded as a force towards conformity. Recently many Europeans have written condemning uniformity. Every man, it is said, is different from his fellow men, and every man should develop in the way most suited to him. The contrary is, to use a word which Western Europeans often use when talking about the nature of Eastern European communist societies, dreariness. It is said that once you endeavour to impose equality, you only succeed in achieving some uniform drabness, without the excellence and variety which are stimulated by inequality and competitiveness.

It is likely too that there has been some modification in European attitudes. It used to be that what was wrong in a society was the existence of extremes: on one hand too much wealth, on the other too much poverty. Europeans have accepted the latter half of this statement, and there is not a single European country which does not, through official government agencies as well as through private initiatives, seek to alleviate poverty and to abolish it in its most extreme forms. However, in spite of taxation policies, death duties and acute class awareness, there is not the same attitude towards extreme wealth. There is even a popular exaltation: when a painting is sold for millions of pounds at auction, when an individual acquires a newspaper or a television chain, when a vast sum of money is given away to charity, Europeans approve rather than disapprove of the revealed accumulation of wealth. As a rule, they do not think it wrong or reprehensible, and they applaud the elements of variety which such excess wealth brings to their societies.

Perhaps this is another way of saying that although liberal democracy, the most dominant European political practice, and socialism, the most persistent European aspiration, have both sought for freedom, social justice and a greater fairness, neither has ever had as its goal any carefully considered plan for equality. Liberal democracy has put its emphasis upon various forms of political freedom. Socialism, as attained in Eastern European states after the war, has emphasised industrialisation, economic growth and an international posture. The abolition of private property, where it has occurred, has not meant that its benefits have been shared out among the population as a whole.

Sometimes, as a result of a desire for greater social justice, further inequalities have been created. To give an example: one of the most important artisanal trades in France was, and remains, that of the bakers. It is still the law that, if a man goes bankrupt, when the settlement is made the baker's bill will be paid first, even if only in part, because the myth still exists that the staple of life is bread. But this was, and still is, the hardest of occupations. Those who worked in a baker's shop traditionally never had any time off. They worked seven days a week and from midnight to noon each day. But in 1936 a law was passed giving one day off a week to workers and shopgirls. This meant that the baker and his wife, the normal arrangement, had to work alone for one day every week. They never had a day off together (unless they closed the shop and allowed their rivals to take over their customers).

Similarly, there are many trade unions which exist in order to preserve the privileged position of certain of their members. In Greece, for example, local trade unions form the basis of all trade-union structure and twenty-one workers in a given company may form a new trade union. In England the train-drivers' union looks back on the days when the locomotive driver was a special type of worker, not to be confused with the clerical employees or porters with whom they served together on the railways. Craft unions, such as printers, used to pass jobs from generation to generation within families. In Sweden, while there is a wage solidarity policy whereby wage-setting is not based on profitability (so that employees with low wages would be subsidising inefficient companies), the wage policy is based upon the principle of the differentiation of wages. The trade-union rule is that there should be fair relations between wages, not wage equality.

It is often argued that equality will be attained by education. Until the emergence of the United States (and in this case they must be seen as an extension of Europe), no continent has given more of its resources to the expansion of education than Europe. This has occurred at all levels and at all times. Europeans understood that if they were to continue their expansion, and if they were to continue their exploitation of their emerging economic power, then there could not be a European base consisting of a mass of undifferentiated and illiterate peasants. This was the economic case for education. But there was also a more humane approach, suggesting that everyone had the right to education, the right to be able to read (especially when, in Protestant Europe, reading was associated with the Bible), that society would become better when ignorance was overcome. There was also a competitive approach. When the French were defeated in 1870 by the Prussians it was immediately said that the cause of Prussian superiority was their educational system; the reforms of the 1880s, instituting free and compulsory education, must be seen in the light of this interpretation. When the British began to appreciate the seriousness of German economic competition throughout the world in the latter part of the nineteenth century, they cited German success in education as something which they could ignore at their peril. The founding of the University of Leeds was, in part, a response to that threat.

Not unnaturally, a preoccupation with education arising from such various reasons did not concentrate on equality. Education can be a force that destroys social barriers, but it can also be a force for the upholding of these barriers. The very fact that systems of education were installed with the name of 'elementary' shows how inequality was encouraged. In a sense there was a parallel between industry and education. A child was placed in a class labelled 'elementary'. Only the stray individual would escape from that category and move up a hierarchical structure. A man is placed in front of a machine. He is there for the rest of his life, and only a stray individual will be able to escape from this and climb a ladder which will lead him to greater freedom and prosperity.

Obviously, within this no-go social area there is movement. West Indians coming to England, Algerians going to France, Turks going to West Germany, are all motivated by the idea that their children will receive a better education in Europe than they would have done in their native country. They have the hope of social mobility in mind. From labourer or shop assistant to clerical worker, technician or manager; and from there upwards to further social strata. But this is not the same thing as equality.

When one talks of equality and hierarchy in Europe today, one must take account of submerged groups. In Western Europe there are the millions of unemployed; there are the immigrants, many of whom live in ghettoes which are badly supplied with social services; there are women who tend to be under-represented in political parties and trade unions, and who are exploited in both Western and Eastern Europe; there are areas of particular countries which are dramatically poorer than other, neighbouring areas, so that living there, or owning property there, is unrewarding. In these senses inequality triumphs. It is not unfair to quote an English source, a Fabian pamphlet published in 1893, and to reflect on how it reads today. 'Even more pathetic than the unemployed male worker and industrial nomad is the workless woman or girl in search of work in a city of great distances. Trudging from shop to factory with thin boots and thinner clothes; with little food, without the support that trade unionism gives to men, lacking the stimulant of association, isolated by her sex, with no organisation, often the victim of bogus registry offices, friendless and alone, she searches for work that slowly comes.'

In many parts of Europe today it is claimed that workers are underpaid: in France that the minimum wage laws are not observed, in Germany that Turkish immigrants are exploited by employers, in Italy and Spain that women employees receive pittances, in England, according to the Low Pay Research Unit, that more than 40 per cent of the workforce are so badly paid that they live in poverty. Naturally a great deal depends upon what one means by being 'underpaid' or what one understands by 'poverty'. Most would argue that there has been an increase in the feeling of injustice, the sense of grievance, which the underprivileged experience, even though there has been an improvement in social welfare. In this sense it can be argued that we are witnessing an increase in class consciousness. But given a long-standing economic crisis and the persistence of unemployment affecting many traditional trades and occupations, and affecting young people in particular, it can also be argued that there has been a decline both in economic welfare and in job opportunity. Thus there is not only relative deprivation, a sense of the world being unjust because one's neighbour is doing better than oneself, but a real deprivation when people are not only without 'the conveniences and amusements of human life' (as Adam Smith put it), but for whom the necessities of life are sometimes in short supply.

It could be that, with the economic crisis of Western Europe and the economic difficulties which Eastern European countries continually experience, we are witnessing a revival of the two nations, the rich and the poor. It could be too that we are witnessing a further complication in class. There is a stratification of societies by profession. People, from within their own professions, tend to look outward to a range of people in similar positions across the world who are practising the same profession. They do not rid themselves of the idea of class and they may well, say, in politics, express themselves in traditional ways, voting for political parties which express their class preoccupations. But they are part of a fresh pecking order, as the credit-card agencies with their special-privilege offers realise. A restaurant, a club, a wine bar can be specially designed for such a group; it can, within a matter of a few weeks, redesign its premises to switch its appeal to another group. Throughout Western Europe there is an ever-increasing army of such people, often loosely described as executives, the most prosperous employed by international corporations.

But while these glossy new horizontal worlds are forming, what happens to the great body of people? It could be that the great forces of these societies – the centralising and unifying forces, which work in both capitalist and non-capitalist societies – will create a huge mass of people at the bottom of the European heap. It will not necessarily be a poverty-stricken mass, although (as we have seen) poverty can be there. It could well be quite a comfortable and well-entertained mass. As is always appropriate in European history, one can turn to the past. More than a hundred years ago, Dostoevsky said of these masses:

> Yes, we shall set them to work, but in their leisure hours we shall make their life a child's game . . . oh, we shall allow them even sin, they are weak and helpless, and they will love us like children because we allow them to sin. The most powerful secrets of their conscience, all they will bring to us and we shall have an answer for all, and they will be glad to believe our answer, for it will save them from the great anxiety and terrible agony they endure at present in making a free decision for themselves.

Herbert Reed, in 1964, looking to the future, said, 'It will be a gay world. There will be lights everywhere except in the minds of men, and the fall of the last civilisation will not be heard above the incessant din.'

The key word today is not 'legitimated sinning', but rather 'triviality'. The masses of population are on the receiving end of opinions, impressions and amusements. They cannot reply or respond effectively. They cannot organise themselves. There is a new unity of Europe expressed by the Eurovision Song Contest, by *Jeux sans Frontières*, by interminable sporting contests and soap operas and now by satellite TV.

But there are some green shoots in a large flat landscape. Throughout Europe one can see the rise of small special-interest or local community groups which are fighting against being stereotyped, taken for granted, forgotten, marginalised. They represent women, the handicapped, one parent families, environmental groups, immigrants, old age pensioners, war veterans, pacifists. They can represent the under-privileged or those who have privileges and who are not prepared to give them up. They can represent a large population which feels oppressed. They can stand up for distant populations for whom they feel a particular sympathy. Europe retains its hierarchical structure but it has also become the home of protest groups.

The Grand Place, Brussels 'In the city, time becomes visible' (Lewis Mumford)

5 · INDIVIDUALS AND COMMUNITIES

The sense of individuality is overwhelmingly European. Christianity is about the salvation of the individual; many aspects of Christianity concern the means whereby an individual person can communicate directly with God. Politics is often about the individual, the rights of man, the right to vote, freedom of speech, the right to work, the right to strike, human rights. Economics is often about an individual taking the initiative and creating wealth, it is also about farmworkers preferring the uncertainty of seasonal labour to the security of personal subservience. The desire to get away alone to the outback, to the High Peaks, to the unknown, is a constant theme in Europe's life and literature.

We find certain phrases, famous in European history, which express this sense. 'Here I stand for I can do no other': Luther's phrase as he defended the propositions he had nailed to the church door of Wittenberg in 1517 is the classic statement of a European individualist. So is 'I disapprove of what you say, but I will defend to the death your right to say it,' usually attributed to Voltaire (but said now not to have been his). 'A self-made man', another European concept, is an arrogant, worldly and individualistic phrase. It has links back to the spirit of Protestantism, and implies that the individual must make his own way, both in the world and with God. 'The greatest thing in the world is to know how to be sufficient unto oneself,' was how Montaigne put it. 'This above all: to thine own self be true, And it must follow, as the night the day, Thou canst not then be false to any man,' said Shakespeare's Polonius, advising his son. These characteristic European touchstones, and similar ones, are frequently to be found in speeches delivered to schools or in collections of maxims used by politicians.

W. H. Auden caught the mood of individuals rejecting the comforts and the crowdedness of European urban life when he wrote:

> The best and worst never stayed here long but sought
> Immoderate soils where the beauty was not so external,
>   The light less public and the meaning of life
> Something more than a mad camp. 'Come!' cried the
>   granite wastes,
>   'How evasive is your humour, how accidental
> Your kindest kiss, how permanent is death.' (Saints-to-be
>   Slipped away sighing.)

Yet it is obvious that individualism is not enough. Christianity is not only about individual salvation; it is also about an organised Church, an established set of beliefs, rules of conduct, the lives of communities. Politics is not only about individual rights, but about the state, about laws, citizenship, authority. In economic matters it is not enough for an individual to be industrious, ambitious and skilful. Capitalism needed more than a few great entrepreneurs; it needed a system and a way of life common to whole groups of men. Imperialism and the expansion of Europe became dependent upon the chancellories of the states, upon the hoisting of flags and the movement of armies and navies.

In Europe there has always been an inherent conflict between the concept of the individual and the necessity for the individual to conform to different sorts of organisations. Jean-Jacques Rousseau was probably the philosopher who was most determined to resolve this dilemma, postulating the idea of man living outside society and being drawn into a situation where he was obliged to work with other men. Man became a creature with a sense of values and a recognition of rights and duties, corrupted by society and by the inequality that society necessarily imposes. The dilemma which Rousseau set out to solve was how the individual could retain moral goodness, maintain freedom and achieve equality while living and working in an organised society.

One can see the same dilemma in a Greek tragedy which has preoccupied European dramatists and poets from Sophocles to Anouilh: that of Antigone. It was used by Hegel to illustrate the difference between different sorts of laws. Antigone follows family law, or divine law, or, if one wishes, individual responsibility, in believing that she should bury her dead brother. Creon, the king, for reasons of state, forbids his burial. Antigone goes to her death because, as an individual, she has defied a political law.

The same dilemma can be explained in an anecdote. Mary Shelley was pressed to send her son to a school 'where they will teach him to think for himself'. 'Oh my God, no,' she replied, 'teach him to think like other people.' Two European aspirations are expressed here (in fact, Mary Shelley sent her son to Harrow and presumably won the argument).

In Europe, as the sense of individualism has been refined and expressed by philosophers and political scientists, the sense of collectivism has also been encouraged and analysed. Some have claimed that the contradictions between the two can never be reconciled: liberty and the cult of the individual cannot go with socialism and the cult of the community. A Spanish North American, George Santayana, claimed that England was the paradise of individuality, eccentricity, heresy, anomalies, hobbies and humours. It could not continue to exist when taken over by those whom he (quite unjustly) chose to call 'scientific blackguards, conspirators, churls and fanatics'. But many others have thought that the individual could maintain his identity and his freedom, if merged within a local community, or a finely tuned liberal state where private and public can cooperate, or a national state where the characteristics of the individual are subsumed within the nation, or conceivably a European community where European individualisms can adapt to both national and international organisations.

Europeans also have a sense of fraternity. The French Revolution took place in the name of 'Liberty, Equality and Fraternity' but, as R. H. Tawney remarked, 'in England liberty and equality have been considered antithetic while fraternity has not been considered at all.' Perhaps this was because liberty had been supported by the broad coalition of classes that had opposed the arbitrary role of the monarchy, while equality in terms of legal and political rights united broad sections of the middle classes and eventually the workers. Fraternity became the watchword of fascist parties, and after the First World War one finds the idea of fraternity being pushed by sentimentalists and nationalists such as d'Annunzio in Italy, Barrès in France, Stefan George in Germany; meanwhile, socialists concentrated on positions of power, on who would control the economy. Yet fraternity and 'camaraderie', fellowship, brotherhood, are part of a European tradition, as those who are from different backgrounds proclaim that they are all 'of the people' and 'brothers beneath the skin'. The old hymn

> The rich man in his castle
> The poor man at his gate
> God made them, high and lowly,
> And ordered their estate

is usually seen as a manifestation of class distinction, but it can also be claimed to be a proclamation of fraternity, comparable to John Donne's 'Never send to know for whom the bell tolls; it tolls for thee.'

Europeans certainly have, in this as in other matters, a sense of difference when compared to non-Europeans. A European working for an international body, such as the United Nations, might be asked to investigate some problem and to prepare a report. That report would probably aim to be objective, in accordance with European tradition, and would say what the individual, according to his understanding and his conscience, had discovered. But the assumption among African and Asian colleagues might well be that the individual was merely presenting what his government, his state, wished him to say. The idea of individual intellectual independence is not taken for granted. Nor was it assumed that this sort of individuality was as admirable and as necessary as Europeans suppose.

It is true that many European values, especially material values, have penetrated the non-European world. Most Africans and Asians serving on international bodies are not averse to the luxuries of American and European hotels or to the many advantages which money brings. But working in their own countries it is easy to come across officials and leaders who are not envious of their European colleagues, who do not think in terms of material benefits, who think that their family is their wealth. This is not, as Europeans would say, choosing the simple life. It is a natural life, far removed from the competitiveness, the demands and the recriminations which the combination of individualism and collectivism has imposed on Europe.

A European watching a village ceremony in Asia, say a funeral or a marriage, something which was not put on for tourists and which was part of long tradition, will be struck by the total absorption of the whole community, by the absence of any awkward, dissident, difficult individuality. The all-embracing community is difficult for Europeans to understand. It arises from community of place, of tribe, of religion, of language. It is received rather than considered, argued about, analysed, thought through. It implies a weak sense of individual responsibility or of rights, a strong sense of communal action and obligation. It can be argued that tribal society is the most permanent and stable type of society, since its sense of kinship, family and blood relationships means that the community sees itself as deriving from the same ancestors. There is a feeling not only of family continuity but of biological continuity. It is continually said that tribalism cannot continue to exist in the modern world, but its presence remains strong, decades after Europeans have foretold its demise.

In Europe one sees three concomitant levels of understanding. There is the local community, the ordinary people, whose viewpoint is limited. Anecdotes abound which illustrate this, showing that in some village no one knew who was the emperor, the king, the Prime Minister (Turgenev's story of meeting a Russian peasant who asked about the British Foreign Secretary, Lord Palmerston, is remembered purely because it is unusual). There is the state community, where people are conscious of the fact that there is an organisation which has encompassed the structuring of social classes and which has established the external ordering of one state towards another, in both military and economic terms. Third, there is an international community – that of the Grand Tour, when it was taken for granted by the upper classes of all nationalities that they should visit the great centres of European culture; when European architects, decorators, sculptors, thought and worked in similar forms, and all Europe thought of the town as a centre of public buildings, with streets and squares laid out in a regular and harmonious pattern; when music was intra-European, with the opera choirs of great cathedrals singing sacred and secular songs; when scientists worked without reference to frontiers.

All three levels persist. There remain those whose horizons are limited, who know and care little for the world that lies beyond their community. There remain the national states. There remains a vestigial sense of the Grand Tour with the tourist's compulsion to visit the Louvre or the Uffizi, to stand in the Piazza San Marco or to stay on a Greek island. But it is obvious that the purely local sense of community is becoming weaker. Television means that a Breton peasant is familiar with the face of the Greek Prime Minister, and the European Community's regulations mean that an Irish dairy farmer knows about the Common Agricultural Policy. Yet the international community has become less meaningful. The twinning of European towns is not the same as Byron's two years on the Grand Tour; a visit to a French civilisation course at the Sorbonne is not of the same order as Milton travelling to meet Grotius and Galileo, or Erasmus visiting Oxford and Cambridge. It is the second, the institution of the European state, that has triumphed.

European states might be said to have begun with the city-states, which both for Hegel and for Weber gave a distinctive quality to European civilisation. They have always been praised. The Greek city-states, especially Athens, are supposed to lie at the origins of democracy. In medieval Italy there were more than two hundred cities which could be described as autonomous, where well-established and wealthy families ruled over a varied collection of classes, factions, wards, guilds, parishes and fraternities. There were city-states in Dalmatia, in southern France, in the Netherlands, in Germany, in Switzerland and as far north as Danzig and Novgorod.

Most of the states disappeared rather easily, some absorbed by their neighbours, some collapsing into anarchy, some (such as Ghent, La Rochelle or Novgorod) suppressed by centralising monarchs, some such as Venice or Hamburg persisting for many years.

From the city-states it is easy to turn to the cities, especially to the great cities that grew from the late nineteenth century onwards. Europe is to be recognised by these establishments; it is with these cities that the inhabitants created their cultural identity. It is, of course, often assumed that city life in the nineteenth century was a story of unmixed woe, with poverty, disease, violence, indifference and dirt stalking the streets, in contrast to a rural image of village life where the poor and the sick were cared for by the church and the squire and happiness reigned. It has also been suggested that there is a sameness in all industrial towns. Manchester, Birmingham, Lille, Roubaix, Essen, Viener Neustadt or Klavno all seem to be surrounded by a uniform drabness, the same smoking chimneys, a similar brutal ugliness. Dickens, in his famous picture of Coketown in *Hard Times*, described the unchanging sameness that existed within the town, the same streets, the same hours, the same work, the same people, every day the same, every hour the same.

But, in fact, violence and poverty were not everywhere, any more than individual cities were all the same. People came and went. Irishmen coming to Liverpool and Birkenhead brought with them their banners and marches, Bretons going to work in Paris settled in the region of Montparnasse, Turks in Berlin settle in a particular part of the city. In these ways a city can be made a success for local loyalties. At the turn of the century Charles Booth, surveying the East End of London, noted how each area had its own atmosphere, its own character and flavour. People treated their local environment as a focal point for their loyalties.

Birmingham is an example of a town which grew rapidly and which encouraged identity and loyalty. Dominated by a great civic

leader, Joseph Chamberlain, it combined a varied economy, a
stimulating diversity of religions, philanthropy and small masters.
With an excellent water supply, acquiring theatres, music-halls, a
symphony orchestra and a university, it had some of the facilities
of a city-state. Like the Paris of Balzac, who showed the life of a
big city which had started as a collection of villages stuck together,
where, he claimed, everyone knew everyone else's affairs and talked
about them. It was just like any country town in France, only
bigger, more exciting, more vital. Like present-day West Berlin,
which has attracted young people from all over Germany because
it seems to have escaped a certain stiffness that exists in the Federal
Republic, and because the young attract the young, it too has
become a place where 'the contagion of numbers' is meaningful.

Not all cities were so successful. When Italy was finally united
in 1870 it seemed natural enough that Rome should be its capital.
Historically it was the inevitable choice. But it was unfortunate.
Rome was a divided city. Those who were loyal to the Pope did
not recognise or approve of unification; there were rivalries among
the aristocracy; more than forty thousand officials descended upon
the town to act as the government, members of parliament had
to be lodged, the government launched a lavish public works
programme in order to make Rome a modern capital city. The
result was a long wave of speculation in land and the construction
of many unfortunate buildings. The resultant high local taxation
made Rome an unpopular place to live in. It was also said that a
few years of Italian rule had done more to destroy Rome than the
barbarians. Rome was not a great industrial centre. It was provincial in culture. Its climate was poor. It was a city where tourists
came to look at the past. Italians could not be loyal to Rome as
they could be to Turin or Milan, Venice or Florence.

Even where cities remained the focus of collective life (one thinks
of Vienna, Prague, Budapest), there were changes in culture, a
certain urban disintegration. The growth of suburbs, the rehousing
of working populations, the electric-grid system, the motorcar,
road-widening, the multiplication of institutions (banks, stores,
offices), authorities who were determined to modernise and speculators who were anxious to make money, all this has invariably
meant the destruction of much that was distinctive in urban civili-

sation. The town no longer attracts loyalty. It is difficult for the inhabitant of the suburbs, of sub-topia, of derelict inner cities, of high-rise flats, of anonymous *pavillons*, shopping precincts, traffic-jammed streets, sprawling office blocks, to identify with these areas. People are interested in their homes, their domestic situation, their gardens when they have them, not in the particular localities where they are situated.

Hence, to solve the dilemma of the individual and the collectivity, there remains the state – in European terms, the nation-state.

Everyone knows what a national state is. It has frontiers, flags, national anthems, passports and government. We associate a national state with a national language, a national history, a national literature and other forms of culture. Part of the national state is ideology, whether this is described as patriotism, loyalty, national selfconsciousness, pride or jingoism; it can be associated with hostility to someone who is exterior to this nationality, a foreigner. The nation-state became the master institution of the modern world; it played a vital part in transforming the economy of Western Europe and in revolutionising the role of Europe in the world. All the activities of Europeans – their technology and inventiveness, their cult of the natural sciences, their understanding of the need to save money and to accumulate capital – had to find the right context. That context was the nation-state. There grew up national banking systems, national markets, even a national drive to succeed. National rivalries increased the tempo of change as the British, the French, the Portuguese and the Dutch chased each other around the Indian Ocean, in and out of the Spice Islands, or fought each other by the Great Lakes of North America. In a continent such as Africa the Europeans, this time including the Belgians, the Germans and the Italians, acquired territories in order to prevent their neighbours and their rivals from doing so.

The very fact that these nation-states fought each other meant an acceleration of technological innovations as each strove to have weapons which were better than the other. It meant too that as each state had to raise money in order to pay for war, taxation systems became more sophisticated, and as the easiest way of raising money is with the consent of the governed, gradually citizens began to gain political rights. The national community thus developed its own sense of kinship, replacing tribalism, feudal-ism, the pre-eminence of the Church, the dominance of the one absolutist ruler.

To the nineteenth-century Italian Mazzini, it was only national-ism, the sense of belonging to one nation, which could bind societies together. When, after the First World War, the peacemakers gath-ered together in Paris to redraw the map of Europe, they had to decide on a principle under which they would act and they chose the principle of nationalism. So the different nationalities, which had once been governed by the Habsburgs of Vienna or by the Sultans of Constantinople, formed their own states in the Balkans or in Central Europe. And the principle of nationality was applied to the defeated state Germany as well, which remained a national state in spite of the French suggestion that Germany should be split up with separate governments in the Rhineland or in the south. For a statesman like General de Gaulle, the nation-state was the only political reality. It was something organic, something which had a life of its own, founded in historic tradition. He saw Europe as a collection of 'indestructible nations', stretching from Gibraltar to the Urals and from Spitzbergen to Sicily.

What is relevant to the position of the individual in Europe is the way in which the power of the nation-state has increased. From being responsible for the defence of the territory from invasions, the state became the authority which resolved internal conflicts and imposed order, and it developed into the organisation which recorded tradition and provided education, information and wel-fare. So far as the individual was concerned, a great bureaucratic organisation was created, which could mean that he was controlled in what he ate and drank, how he brought up his children, what life-style he adopted. In general terms this bureaucracy was a professional body, recruited in a specific way according to tra-ditions and rules, forming a formidable meritocracy. On occasions it was responsible to elected bodies, legislatures and parliaments, but there it came into contact with the other characteristic of the nation-state, the political party. Each state had its own political parties, with their own particular means of organising support, their own vocabulary, principles and objectives.

Thus the nation-state has been a huge success. Men have gone to their deaths in its name. People have made immense sacrifices because they are patriotic and believe in their national flag, their national ritual and rhetoric. National heritage has been enshrined in museums, commemorative dates and ceremonies. Children have been brought up to believe that their country, their nation, is superior to all others. Educated and sophisticated people will weep with joy if their national team wins some sporting event, and may even go on the rampage if their team loses. Crimes are committed in the name of the nation against other nations, against those who have served the nation badly or falsely. 'Our country right or wrong' was said by an American, but it is a very European attitude. 'My country, how I love my country,' may not really have been the dying words of William Pitt, but the legend has persisted because English people, like other Europeans, admire and take comfort from the patriotism of their leaders.

However, the success and the reputation of the European state have become tarnished. For one thing, because of its own inadequacies. For another, because the European model has been applied to new nations outside Europe with some lack of success.

In both, the starting point of disillusion has been that few of the so-called nation-states are genuine nation-states. That is to say that the frontiers of the state's territories and the boundaries of a homogeneous ethnic community hardly ever coincide. The inhabitants of the state do not possess an identical national culture. In Europe, the Germany which Bismarck created included Poles, Danes and the inhabitants of Alsace and Lorraine who had formerly been part of France. In Great Britain there were the Welsh who spoke a different language, the Scots who had a different legal system, the Irish who fought to break away and live independently. In the states which succeeded the Habsburg and Ottoman Empires, there is the most remarkable confusion of ethnic and language groups. Slav, Teuton and Magyar all live hugger-mugger, while a Turkish minority still strives to maintain its cultural identity in Bulgaria. It is true that at times there are minorities which, for geographical reasons, do not impair the cultural unity of the state. This is the case, for example, with the Lapp and Karelian minorities in Norway, Sweden and Finland. But it is only a minority of European nation-states which can claim to be fully nation-states, such as Portugal, Greece, Poland, Holland and Denmark. Outside Europe, in the new nations, the frontiers established by the former colonial powers seem to have been drawn with a school ruler in straight, meaningless lines, so that they do not contain people of common culture, but rather peoples of a number of different cultures who were placed in a similar political situation because of the patterns of European conquest. Hence many of these states, once they acquired independence, found themselves faced with violent secession movements, as in Pakistan, Zaire, Nigeria and Sri Lanka.

In Europe itself there are other reasons why the idea of the nation-state seems to have failed. It had always been believed that men and women were brothers and sisters to each other. Certain myths persisted. It was believed, for example, that during the 1914–18 war (and this was always regarded as the worst of all wars because the man-to-man nature of the conflict was so obvious) soldiers had shown friendship to each other in spite of official, governmental orders. It was said that a number of French soldiers in their trench caught cold, and that each time they sneezed the German soldiers in a nearby trench shouted out 'Bless you.' There were stories of English and German soldiers playing football together in the no man's land between the trenches, and everyone was brought up to believe in the Christmas Day when canticles and carols were sung and when good wishes and greetings were sent from trench to trench. But the essence of the nation-state is, it was claimed, to deny this essential fraternity of the human race. It claims authority and it claims exclusive loyalty. Nationalism will reject from the embrace of goodwill and reject from brotherhood those who happen to live on the other side of the river. The pretensions of the nation-state are enormous and they are backed by the ultimate sanction of life or death.

In 1945 it seemed that the embodiment of nationalism was the Nazi state. It advanced its claims of being one state and one people under one ruler to that of representing one master race. This unleashed further national hatreds, as French, Dutch, Norwegians, Poles and others rejoiced when they learned of the bombing and the destruction of the German cities. Such toleration of conflict had always existed among tribal organisations. But the disorder had been limited, sometimes only ritual. With the powerful discipline and the conformity which the modern nation state had been able to impose, and with the destructive power of weapons in the twentieth century, such warfare brought Europe to the edge of destruction. In 1918 it had been claimed that the cause of war had been secret diplomacy (and much of this was the result of having nation-states); in 1945 it was claimed that the war had been caused by nationalism, orchestrated by the institution of the nation-state. In 1945 it seemed that with the existence and the future development of nuclear weapons, the intolerance of the nation-state could only mean conflict which would bring about the annihilation of humanity. Therefore it was felt that some alternative to the nation-state had to be found, and in particular, since the wars of 1870, 1914 and 1939 had centred around Franco-German conflict, it seemed that it was in the interests of all Europe that some way out of this pattern of hostility had to be devised.

Then most important of all perhaps, it became apparent that the nation-state could not remain the master institution in economic terms. There was a new economic universe, compared to which national markets were pitifully inadequate. It was all very well for Holland, and then for Britain, to establish themselves as great economic powers working from a small base, because they were the first in the field, and the world was at their feet. But when Germany became a great economic power it found that it could not expand its national market without embarking upon a policy of conquest, which was the essence of the two World Wars.

It is appropriate that the first direct attack on the nation-state principle should have occurred over Germany. It was over the future of post-war Germany that the two superpowers, the United States and Soviet Russia, entered into conflict. Russia was determined to exact ten billion dollars of reparations from Germany, and to participate in the exploitation of the industries of the Ruhr. The Americans believed that this concealed a Soviet desire to dominate the whole of Germany, and Stalin was reported as saying, in the spring of 1946, that 'All of Germany must be ours, that is Soviet, communist.' The American riposte was the Marshall Plan, a spending programme to refloat the economy of Europe. The result was the creation of the two Germanies, Western and Eastern, effectively from 1948. It is true that the French government, with its desire to obtain security for the future from some possible resurgence of Germany, played its part, but no one put forward the argument that it was wrong to divide Germany because a German nation – a historical, ethnic, linguistic group – existed. The French writer François Mauriac was later to say, with appropriate cynicism, that France liked Germany so much that it was glad to see two of them.

The very fact that the United States was intervening directly in European affairs which were so distant from home was also a comment on the national state. This is because, although originally without tribal or national antecedents, the political experiment that was America took on, as time went by, the characteristics of a national community. All the characteristics of a national state were planted and grew. There was the flag, the anthems, the school, the long history which was shown in a variety of telling and incisive ways. The experience of the Civil War, the story of expansion westward, the idea that America was unique and stood for something universal: all this made for an Americanism which had the pride of European nationalism. Furthermore, protected by two oceans, endowed with a land that was ideal for farming and rich with resources, equipped with a continuously expanding population and internal market, uninhibited by the fetters of tradition which marked European countries, America was destined to be the ideal community. America could ignore the rest of the world and enjoy its privileges as a nation. The political principle of isolationism so prominent in the period between the wars was the expression of this sentiment. But when, in 1914 and in 1939, rival nation-states disputed who should gain control in Europe, America could not hold aloof; just as when in 1929 world trade fell to a third of its volume and unemployment soared, America was in the centre of a world depression. American interests could not be contained inside the nationalist, isolationist formula. American patriotism remained undimmed. The message of the young and radical President John Fitzgerald Kennedy at his inauguration ceremony was traditional in its rhetoric and in its implications. 'Ask not what your country can do for you; ask what you can do for your country.' One can have the experience of walking down a street with an American academic, discussing the natures of different countries, who will suddenly turn to you and say, 'I love America.' Such words do not easily trip off the tongue of a European academic, and are impossible from an English academic. American patriotism remains young, direct, uncomplicated. Yet the United States sees itself as beyond frontiers, a world power rather than a national power, the defender of a system of rights and principles which go well beyond national self-interest. America cannot contract out of the global society which the nation-states had been instrumental in building.

As far as Russia is concerned, the question is more complex. Soviet Russia is clearly a multi-national state (with Russians making up only slightly over half of the population). Soviet Russia is also, theoretically at least, a Marxist state – one which regards the traditional nation-state purely as a device to protect capitalism within that state – and therefore, in the name of international socialism and the interests of the working class throughout Europe, Russia is no friend to nationalism and the nation-state. In practice Russia has shown an unmistakable hostility to manifestations of nationalism as they have appeared in the communist states of Eastern Europe (especially Poland, Hungary, Czechoslovakia and Yugoslavia). Yet it is apparent that a Soviet chauvinism exists. After 1917 the Soviet state became a national state like any other, protecting its territory and its interests. The pact which the Soviet government signed with Hitler in 1939 was proof of this. Russian resistance to the German invasion after 1941 was organised on the basis of patriotism and the legendary figures of Russia's historic past were marshalled to support Mother Russia. Yet it remains true that Russian governments still see the USSR as the fatherland of workers everywhere, the vanguard socialist state, the most powerful opponent of international capitalism. As such Soviet Russia, like the United States, is more than a nation-state.

When African and Asian peoples began to intensify their demands for independence, it was customary for Europeans to see this as the equivalent outside Europe of what had happened within Europe. Indians, Indonesians, Tunisians, Nigerians were simply doing what Germans, Italians, Czechs and Serbs had done in the previous century. In spite of opposition, uncertainty and confusion, it became accepted by most European colonial governments that it was only right that these territories should accede to independence; even when the colonial government had fought a war to prevent this from happening, there were some among their fellow-countrymen who opposed the war and supported independence. The last legacy of the West to the new nations was that this independent state should be a nation-state, and those who gained independence were called 'the new nations'.

The transition, even where there had been conflict, was usually simple and straightforward, and took place in a European manner. In former British colonies there were bewigged judges in their robes, a parliamentary mace imitated from that of the House of Commons, and a bound volume of Erskine May's book on parliamentary practice and procedure. In the case of former French colonies there were speeches, French-style military fanfares and many references to the universality of French culture. The new leaders, who spoke the European languages of the colonial governments with distinction and ease, who dressed elegantly in European clothes, and who had actually been educated at the Sorbonne, the London School of Economics or the Massachusetts Institute of Technology, were in the tradition of European government. Although many of them had seen the inside of European jails and although many had known suffering in the struggle for independence, they adopted (at least at first) an attitude of tolerance towards their former rulers (which many Europeans would like to describe as very European). In order to gain independence rapidly they often permitted important European interests to remain in their territories, and they welcomed the continued presence of the ex-colonial administrators, experts or teachers.

But all this meant only that an independent state had been acquired. What was necessary was to build a nation. How could one make a nation starting from scratch? The belief that one can make a simple progression from tribe to nation or from colony to sovereign state has not been sustained. The presence of frontiers, passports, European-style armed forces (with weapons sometimes happily supplied at a profit by the former imperialists, sometimes supplied with political intent by other countries), a full-scale television system and an airline (neither of which can always be afforded or justified economically), together with flags, anthems, political parties and forms of parliament, may constitute the paraphernalia of a state but not of a nation.

One of the leaders of these new nations – the Ivory Coast – posed the problem. 'In a country which has successively seen seven languages and seven different cultures, and in which a score of political regimes have done their utmost to reduce the natives to the rank of second-class citizens and to destroy even the memory of their predecessors, a term such as "national culture" is scarcely an adequate one to use.'

The mix of the inherited methods of thought and procedure, and the idea of the modern bureaucratic state with taxation, economic planning, defence and decision-making at the centre of a government's preoccupations, is a difficult one. It seeks to bring together an individualistic, rational approach and a non-individualistic communitarianism. Tom Mboya, one of the leaders of Kenyan nationalism and a prominent member of the Luo tribe, wanted to introduce the principle of one man one vote into Kenya while it was still under British rule. An English journalist asked how he could justify giving the vote to people who could neither read nor write and whose horizons were limited to the village or the small town. Mboya replied that his grandfather could neither read nor write, but that he was the wisest man that he knew. 'If ever,' he said, 'I have a problem, I will always consult my grandfather.'

This story illustrates the difficulty of bringing together the age-old tradition of the wisdom of tribal elders with the hustle and bustle and confusions of modern political systems. The same difficulty can be seen when we look at African universities. Ibadan, in Nigeria, is a transplanted British university with a vast rolling campus, not unlike Exeter University or the University of Sussex. Dakar, in Senegal, is a French university. They both exist apart from the societies which surround them, almost like the English clubs and the French *cercles* of the old colonial days.

These new states, with few exceptions, are made up of a mosaic of peoples, each with distinct linguistic and colonial features; they have their own histories, sometimes their own values, often their own traditional institutions. Under colonial rule they may have existed together in an economic sense, but they did not integrate together socially or politically. These states, which encompass plural societies and subcultural groups, are invariably poor, and the sharing out of scarce resources becomes a dangerous rather than a difficult task when regions, tribes, groups, can claim that they are unfairly treated.

Post-colonial inheritance still poses its problems. Colonial governments sometimes favoured one particular ethnic group and used it in their administration, as the French favoured the Kabyles in Algeria, the British relied on the Baganda in Uganda or the Tamils in Sri Lanka. With independence, resentment against these formerly privileged groups was given a free hand, and these conflicts added to the impossibility of a government being able to count upon the natural loyalty of the majority of its citizens.

Some states have tried to solve these problems by creating a ruler who can be identified with the state. This is a method familiar to Europeans. Any European attending a mass open-air rally in Indonesia arranged for President Suharto was immediately re-minded of a Nuremberg rally addressed by Hitler. The president swept in with all the apparatus of a modern single-party state ruler: a huge car, bodyguards, outriders, soldiers with machine guns, Cabinet ministers a due step behind him. As he mounted the rostrum, a great ululating cry arose from the crowd as solid as the 'Heil Hitler's of the rallies. But in Asia it was different. The crowd shouted, 'Papa President, Papa President.' A hard-faced, restless-eyed politician had been presented, absorbed and accepted as the father of a huge, artificially constructed, national and nationalistic family. A European found it difficult to accept this as right.

It was much the same with the self-styled Emperor Bokassa, with his admiration for Napoleon and his gold throne, or for General Amin, wearing English and Scottish military uniforms and decor-ations to which he was not entitled. Europeans too find it hard to accept the harsh nationalist ideologies and strident propaganda which are the substance of much political activity, sometimes put out by mass political parties or by political leaders who have captured the means of communication and who control the news-papers and the airwaves.

But Europeans should recognise that they are to a considerable extent contemplating their own heritage. After Italy had been united as one state, d'Azeglio remarked in a frequently quoted phrase, 'We have made Italy, now we must make Italians.' The paradox of the situation is that at a time in the middle of the twentieth century, when it was becoming generally accepted that the nation-state was not a success, this concept of the nation-state was claimed by, and foisted on, the Third World. The assumption was that the only real state was a nation-state and the only way by which a nation could realise itself was to become a state. The very omnibus term 'nation-state' obscures the intricate relations between the ethnic, linguistic and cultural aspects of nation and the legal, organisational and structured aspects of state.

Yet the fact remains that most educated and politically aware people identify themselves with some sort of national culture, and commit themselves to it as individuals. Even in something as international as music, where there is no barrier of understanding and no sense of exclusivity, it is taken for granted that the music of Elgar and Vaughan Williams has qualities that are notably English, while the music of Debussy and Ravel is typically French, that of Schubert German, that of de Falla Spanish, that of Verdi Italian, while Dvořák and Smetana are clearly Slavonic. From these assumptions there is no going back.

In the Third World there is no going back either. One of the characteristics of an independent state is admission to the United Nations where the tiniest of states has a vote, so that the Seychelles or Gambia or Equatorial Guinea are formally rated equally with Japan. The international situation protects small states from conquest, and the international economic situation means that size is no longer a criterion for economic strength or viability. Hence the Third World states strive, often by force, to preserve their unity, and experiment with methods of government which are personalist, populist, neo-administrative elites, or variations of these.

In Europe too there is an atmosphere of experiment in the air. For a time it was noticeable how young people rejected the idea of social status, of getting and spending and all the forms of aggression and casting-off which are associated with those attitudes. For some two decades there was a new sort of Grand Tour – to India, to

Nepal, to those places where a more serene type of spirituality might be found. In Europe itself one came across eastern religions, a new interest in mysticism, meditation, the spiritual teaching of eastern gurus. There is still a vogue for non-European medical practice which standard medical science finds difficult to explain, such as acupuncture. Young people in places like Amsterdam invaded areas of property which they did not own and settled there in densely populated squats, apparently defying European traditions of respecting property rights and the accepted work ethic. An internal means of rejection was to seek a kind of transcendence via drugs or, more publicly, to assert individualism by what at first seemed to be totally non-conformist hair styles and clothes (but which inevitably became a conventional pattern and style). Doubtless many aspects of violence and hooliganism which exist in various forms and degrees in most European societies can be considered among these manifestations of individuals who do not find that they fit into existing collectives.

But there have been other developments. One is the development of further separatist nationalisms. Curiously enough some of these nationalisms aimed, and aim, at breaking up the oldest established nation-states such as Britain, France, Spain and Switzerland. The demand for the absorption of Northern Ireland into the Irish Republic and for an independent Scotland, like the movements of Corsicans, Bretons, Basques and Jura separatists, may never be successful and may vary in strength from year to year. But they represent a general phenomenon. When one considers other movements, which are less clearly separatist but which exist as means whereby individuals find fulfilment in a collectivity, one must count the Welsh, some Cornish, some Genevans, the Catalans and even a construct such as Occitania (in southern France). Possibly too one must see areas which once thought in terms of separatism such as Sicily, Sardinia, the South Tyrol and the Val d'Aosta, or Bavaria as sleeping volcanoes which could erupt.

It has usually been thought that these movements could be satisfied by the process of devolution or by granting a special status to the region concerned. In other words, by tinkering with the machinery of state. This is a process which has been going on in eastern Europe too.

When the Bolsheviks succeeded to power in Russia they succeeded to a despotism which controlled millions, and which held them together by a mixture of force, mysticism, devotion to the Tsar and bureaucracy. It was Imperial Russia which had succeeded Holy Russia. Under the Bolsheviks, the ramshackle Tsarist empire of vast distances, corruption, pieties and uncertainties was converted into a more compact state. The needs of defence and modernisation called for a centralised system of administration and economic planning which embodied the will of the Communist Party and the government. Difficulties were met by increased authoritarianism, and failures were attributed to sabotage. This was the model of socialist planning which was imposed on Poland, the German Democratic Republic, Hungary, Czechoslovakia, Romania and Bulgaria after 1945.

Within Russia the sense of crisis and the needs of war may have caused this regime to be widely accepted. It is curious to note that Andrei Sinyavsky, later to become an early dissident, distanced himself in his youth from the characteristics of Western Europe. In about 1950 he wrote, 'Christianity has been going downhill ever since the Renaissance, ever since it made personal salvation the only thing that mattered. Modern Christianity is individualist; communism is concerned with the good of mankind, so its moral meaning is higher.' But the death of Stalin in 1953 and the 'secret' report of Khrushchev to the Twentieth Congress changed the situation, and there developed the long period of *samizdat* and dissidence. But more particularly there came about a realisation of the need for economic change within the framework of bureaucratic control. From Khrushchev onwards, while it was accepted that basic economic decisions always had to be taken by the central government, it was a matter of discussion whether the individual decisions about consumption or the size of an enterprise's output should be planned within the socialist economy. From Khrushchev to Gorbachev, the discussion on political liberty within the state apparatus has continued.

The economic planning systems of the eastern European states have been in constant change since their establishment. As in the Soviet Union a principal reason was unsatisfactory growth rates. Words like New Economic System and New Economic Mechanism have become familiar, both indicating forms of regulated market economies. But in a country such as Czechoslovakia which had, unlike Russia, experienced European democratic values, the events of 1968–69 went far beyond questions of economic performance but sought to re-adjust political organisation. Socialism had abolished the fundamental contradiction of capitalist society, that between capital and labour. What was necessary was to allow different interests to flourish and to be represented in a socialist society which would not be monolithic. There is no reason to believe that in Hungary in 1956, and in Poland throughout the 1980s, the same modest aspirations were not present. That is to say, that there should be a choice between different political models of socialism.

The sentiment of being involved with new developments is expressed by the scientist Professor Lohs from East Germany, a notable spokesman for his country. He is, of course, aware of the atrocities of the German past. He claims that in the German Democratic Republic one is beginning to be patriotic in a new way – as a factor in peace, as part of a vast European community, as part of communication with all the other states of Europe. 'We are all together, the Europeans, in this community of Fate,' he says.

Sir Walter Scott wrote:

> Breathes there the man, with soul so dead,
> Who never to himself hath said,
> 'This is my own, my native land'?

There is no reason to believe that this is no longer true. But perhaps it is not true in the same way as when Scott wrote, a century and a half ago. The individual, the community, the nation are all changing, and their relationships are forming new patterns.

Sopron, western border of Hungary 'The tapestry of history has no point at which you can cut it and leave the design intelligible' (Dom Gregory)

6 · THE OVER-ARCHED CONTINENT

Europe was mutilated after the Second World War. It sustained two serious losses: its colonial empires, and Eastern Europe.

There were many reasons why the colonial empires went. Undoubtedly Britain felt unable, in 1945, to fight a war in India simply in order to retain it within the British Commonwealth. Britain was not strong enough, and she was tired of war. France, fighting similar colonial revolutions in Indo-China and in Algeria, demonstrated the tragic difficulties of such a course. As General de Gaulle came to see the Algerian problem in 1958: the position of France in Europe, and in the world, would be immeasurably weaker if its army was condemned to fight an endless colonial war. But behind the realities of military and economic weakness, there lurked a European preoccupation with human rights. Britain had always envisaged a day when India would be self-governing, and the principle of the Commonwealth was one of free and voluntary adherence to the organisation. A battle to subject India or other possessions would have unleashed a political storm both at home and in the Dominions; and it would have been difficult to justify after a great war fought in the name of liberty. The United States would certainly not have supported such an action. In France, the wars in both Indo-China and Algeria aroused violent domestic opposition; however, the former was easily forgotten by the majority of the population, while the latter became a special case, as there were a million Algerian non-Moslems who presented themselves as French, and demanded protection.

However, in spite of bloodshed, in spite of the complications of the British in Cyprus or the Belgians in the Congo or the Dutch in Indonesia, the process of decolonisation was rapidly accomplished. One realised how short the British presence in, for example, Uganda had been, and how comparatively recently the French had conquered Madagascar. One saw too how easily the loss of these territories was assimilated. There was, and there remains, a certain nostalgia. A French pop star recalls Oran, the blue sea and the blue sky, singing, 'No, we have not forgotten'; countless films depict the British Raj; men in Belgium and in Holland recall in bewildered wonderment how they, as isolated individuals, ruled over immense territories. But nostalgia is not neurosis. There is no real controversy over the end of empires. The separation of Eastern and Western Europe is a much more painful and serious mutilation. Poland and Hungary were European states; the Polish and Magyar nations were closely associated with the defence of Christianity; Czechoslovakia was a creation of the peacemakers at Versailles in 1919 supported by the work of Western European historians, and Czech leaders became highly respected figures in London, Paris and Geneva. Had there been a referendum in these countries after the last war, it seems almost certain that they would have rejected membership of the Soviet bloc. (Romania and Bulgaria were different, as their national development was complicated by ethnic and religious differences, and by their experience of fascism between the wars.)

The nature of government in this Eastern bloc was determined by Moscow's claim that Marxism-Leninism is a universal and scientific doctrine which can be applied to all socialist countries irrespective of their past histories, and by Moscow's assertion that since the Soviet Union is the oldest, most developed and most powerful socialist state it has the right to oversee and interpret the application of this doctrine. National communist parties existed, but they were compelled to remember that whatever their particular interests or preoccupations they were responsible to all socialist countries, and to the worldwide communist movement led by the Soviet Union.

Development in Eastern European states was slow and uneven. A new class of intellectuals came to the fore, who were versed in the ways of technological and bureaucratic societies and whose expertise suggested that considerable organisational changes were necessary. There were movements in favour of change within the communist parties themselves, since a section of the membership and the apparatus found themselves denied elite status. A large part of the working class appeared to be under-privileged; the wage claims of agricultural and unskilled workers (including many women and young people) were persistently rejected or denied. Within these movements of dissatisfaction there were traditional intellectuals who thought in terms of human rights and in terms of Europe. The Hungarian tradition goes back a thousand years to the first king, Stephen, who had to choose between the pagan tradition and the new Christian ideology. He chose Christianity. Hungarian intellectuals have always interpreted that as the choice for Europe, and are insistent that their country is a part of Europe. In Poland, the Catholic tradition binds the country to Europe (even more so now that there is a Polish Pope).

The mutilation of Europe would have been much greater if Austria had been annexed to the Eastern bloc, as seemed likely at one point. It would have been unthinkable that Vienna should be isolated from Western Europe. The position of Finland, too, was in doubt for some time.

With such an extension of Soviet power and influence, either attained or threatened, it is not unnatural that Western Europe became preoccupied with defence problems and relied on the continued presence of an American army and air force. Perhaps it was this very preoccupation with defence that made Western Europe less aggressive. The last great act of European aggression was the attack on Egypt in the Suez campaign of 1956. (The French fought on in Algeria until 1962, and there have been minor flurries of French military activity since then in Chad and elsewhere, but these are isolated cases.) Within Europe, for more than forty years, the intertribal wars which destroyed so much and so many in the past have ceased. Their empires gone and their continent divided, Western Europeans had little alternative but cooperation.

The most dramatic form of cooperation has been the European Economic Community. The unification of Europe had been advocated by philosophers and statesmen for centuries. The Quaker William Penn (founder of Pennsylvania) had called for the establishment of a European Parliament as early as 1650. The German Romantic writer Novalis and the socialist-inclined Comte de Saint-Simon had looked back on the days when Christian Europe had formed one nation, and forward to the days when free trade would make Europe an economic community. Both Napoleon and Hitler had attempted, in their different ways, to unite Europe under French or German hegemony, projects which had proved unacceptable to other European powers and which had been devoid of idealism. It was in the twentieth century, firstly with a pan-European movement led by Count Coudenhove-Kalergi, and then with Aristide Briand's speech to the League of Nations in 1929, that the idea of a European Federal Union took on a more specific shape. The French Foreign Minister, who pursued his idea with some tenacity, suggested that the prospect for Europe (and he meant all the European states who were members of the League of Nations) was 'to unite in order to live and prosper'. He claimed that the peoples of Europe had shown their feelings clearly in supporting these proposals, but in this he was almost certainly wrong. The British, the Spaniards and the Dutch were considering their colonial empires. The Germans, the Poles, the Czechs and the Hungarians thought that there should be a revision of the Treaty of Versailles before any new arrangements could be made. The whole idea foundered, and the joke prospered that the most that could be hoped for was a common European postage stamp.

However, it is interesting that while Briand's plan involved the merging of all European nationalities into a United States of

Europe, his major concern was Franco-German relations, which had been his starting point as Foreign Minister some years earlier. The same occurred on 9 May 1950, when the French Foreign Minister Robert Schuman announced his plan to put all Franco-German coal and steel production under a common authority. This came about, not so much because there was any vital idealism for creating Europe, but because France had not succeeded in preventing or delaying the economic recovery of Germany and it looked as if Germany was about to resume her role as Europe's industrial giant. By putting the coal and steel industries under a High Authority it would be impossible for Germany to create an economic power which would be dangerous to France, or make an alliance with the Soviet Union. Germany would be bound economically and politically into the structure of Western Europe, and so would France who, equally, would not be able to take up the traditional option of a Franco-Russian alliance.

A British diplomat of the time, Oliver Harvey, believed that while France was searching for security she was also thinking first and foremost about Europe. This meant that the French were conscious of the great historical and cultural values and were thinking of a high civilisation. They were anxious lest those values be submerged in some wider association which would be dominated by the USA and possibly by other overseas powers.

Significantly, the two leading statesmen in this negotiation were Schuman, who was from Alsace (and who had served in the German army during the 1914 war), and Adenauer, who was a Catholic from the Rhineland. It was thus a Continental arrangement, and one which rapidly gained the assent of the Dutch (with some mild protests), Belgians, Luxembourgeois and Italians. But the British were suspicious and hostile. They thought that a European union ought to be Atlantic, and that the United States should be part of it. They were opposed to the idea of a High Authority which would supersede the powers of Parliament. Their destiny lay with the Commonwealth and with some special relationship with the United States.

In this kind of negotiation one can see many of the characteristics of Europe, such as the tendency of one European country to despise another. The British, in 1950, looked down on the French and doubted that the French could ever succeed in realising their plans. Many Germans who opposed the French plan thought it betrayed the potential economic strength of Germany and placed it at the service of French diplomacy. The left wing in France thought the plan was an acceptance of capitalism and an attempt to squeeze the Soviet Union out of Europe; others believed that this was the only way of keeping American influence at bay. Smaller states were worried about competition from a united Franco-German combine, and the Dutch, who have the strongest tradition of independence, made some protestations about their sovereign independence being interfered with by a High Authority.

A duality in all this is clear. On one hand there was an idealism: war between European states must be ended, the European heritage and identity had to be cultivated. On the other hand there was a realism: would Europe fall into the familiar pattern in which Germany became economically powerful, made treaties with the Soviet Union, began a fourth war with France? French diplomacy, therefore, is severely practical, traditional, self-centred.

But there was a bomb lying in the centre of the Schuman Plan. The man who probably inspired it, Jean Monnet, claimed that as it stood (in 1951) it was an anomaly, a supra-national body in a community organised on predominantly nationalist lines. If this entity ever came into being it could not remain static; it must, he said, 'either perish or infect the whole of the rest of the community'. The French intention, or this Frenchman's intention, was that it should do the latter, and the idea of moving forward from the pooling of steel and coal production to a wider European community (which eventually was signed up and came into being on 1 January 1958) was present in the minds of many people who revelled in their idealism. This idealism suggested a revival of the Europe of Charlemagne, a Europe that would be Christian, anti-communist, cultured, peaceful, humane. But others saw in this Europe something essentially materialistic, becoming within a few years of its foundation the world's greatest trading power, the biggest exporter and buyer of raw materials, the area where capitalism thrived and made money for its followers. Within each national state there were many, probably a majority, who saw nothing

visionary or idealistic in the Community, only a means of insti-
tutionalising wealth.

The British Labour Party had no doubts. In a pamphlet published
in June 1950 it stated its conviction that people in Britain were not
European. 'In every respect except distance we in Britain are closer
to our kinsmen in Australia and New Zealand on the far side of
the world than we are to Europe. We are closer in language and
in origins, in social habits and institutions.' The Labour Party was
not alone in this attitude. The Conservative Party could not accept
that some authority beyond the Channel would decide whether or
not British pits and steel works would close. There was a general
feeling that Britain had played a particular role in the war. Britain
had stood alone in 1940, fighting against Germany. The rest of
Europe had collapsed, or collaborated with Germany. Britain was
in a privileged position, not like the rest of Europe, secure in its
special position in the Commonwealth and its special relationship
with the United States.

The same argument applied in matters of European defence,
even though the British government was easily convinced that
Soviet policy was to undermine the economies of Western Europe
and that it was necessary to create an anti-Soviet system. But when,
a few months after Robert Schuman's initiative, in October 1950
the French Prime Minister René Pleven proposed the creation of a
European army, with a European Defence Community controlling
it, Britain refused to join. British objections, in the long tradition of
European diplomacy, were concerned with details: such a scheme
would take too long to implement, it had been badly conceived
and hastily presented. But fundamentally, the British objection was
to the wider pressure to form a federal Europe. Britain could only
join this Europe if it was prepared to give up its non-European
commitments and if it was prepared to identify itself with the
strongly Catholic, Christian-Democratic element in power. Both
concessions were unacceptable; it seemed better to British statesmen and to public opinion that Britain should rely on the Anglo-
American alliance.

It is perhaps significant that at this time of British isolation from
movements towards European unity, Britain was also isolated
intellectually. Everywhere in Europe there was a great interest in

Marxism. There was a consciousness of the shortcomings of Western societies. It seemed that those who should have stood for
Western values had failed. Guilt about the past, recollections of
the hopes of those who had died in the war, unease about the
injustices of Western society, a preoccupation with the uncertainties and dangers of the future, all led to a great discussion. It was
a period of rival cultural congresses, of petitions and campaigns
when many new literary magazines came into being. There were
Marxists who were so attached to the Soviet Union that they
felt that to criticise it would be tantamount to working against
mankind. There were Marxists who were independent, who supported the Yugoslav version of communism or who were prepared
to call for an investigation into Soviet labour camps. There were
existentialists; there were those who sought to liberalise the Catholic Church and to associate it with the proletariat, those who
wished to demythologise the Protestant faith, those who discussed
whether it was possible to be a Catholic and at the same time a
communist. There were many schools of thought, controversies,
fads, groups, modes of intellectual enthusiasm. But in England
none of this happened. There was neither cultural despair nor
ideological ambition. If many English people observed the French
literary scene with admiration and spoke with bated breath about
Sartre and Camus, and if those English people fortunate enough
to live in towns where it was possible to see the new Italian cinema
did so with enthusiasm, the effect of these experiences was minimal.
The post-war decade in Britain knew no outstanding group or
trend. The most respected writers, such as T. S. Eliot, E. M.
Forster, Graham Greene, Evelyn Waugh and George Orwell, were
renowned for their individualism. Otherwise they had little in
common and they owed even less to their colleagues in Europe. It
is curious to think that the war may have made Britain reluctant
to accept that it was part of Europe.

   It is curious too to reflect that at the time when a new concept
of Europe was beginning to develop, the post-war period was
filled with violent national animosities. The liberation of German
concentration camps such as Dachau and Buchenwald and the
discovery of the grisly brutality that had reigned there, the realisation of how the Germans had behaved in countries which they had

occupied, the revelations of the Nuremberg trials, all continued to inspire a hatred of Germany. For years afterwards any big parade in Paris was attended by some Buchenwald survivors, dressed in the distinctive striped uniform that had been worn there. Any suggestion of German rearmament aroused widespread hostility, and when in the late 1950s a few German soldiers took part in manoeuvres on French soil some people regarded it as scandalous. The British, who in general shared the French hostility to the Germans, came in for criticism when certain well-intentioned people, worried at the shortage of food in post-war Germany, attempted to persuade others to send their chocolate rations to the Germans. Many continentals remarked that it was evident that Britain had not experienced a German occupation.

Naturally the Germans resented this hostility and claimed that they, as a nation, were being blamed for the crimes committed by a small number of Nazis. Adenauer never forgave Churchill for his phrase, 'The Germans are either at your throat or at your feet.' As late as 1956, when the British historian Elizabeth Wiskemann wrote a study of Germany's eastern neighbours in which she assumed that the German provinces occupied by Poland and by Czechoslovakia in 1945 would not be returned to Germany, there was an outcry and wild allegations were made against her and against England. The French occupying forces, both in Germany and in Austria, were accused of bad and selfish behaviour and were described as 'scented Russians'.

The British made themselves unpopular in both Italy and Greece, where they were accused of behaving as if they were in their old colonial territories. Spain was ostracised by everyone. There were controversies over the ways in which Sweden and Switzerland had interpreted neutrality and whether or not they might have adopted a more generous policy towards refugees. There was resentment in Britain and France against the Belgian king who had abruptly surrendered his army in 1940, but this was probably drowned in the political dissent which marked Belgian national life after the liberation, and the purely Belgian controversy which surrounded the king (reminding others of the old story that when a Belgian is travelling by train at night and hears the sound of violent quarrelling, he knows he has reached home). Everywhere one heard of the callousness of indiscriminate American bombing and every-where one heard tales of the primitive savagery of the Russian troops.

There was no popular sense of Europe. This was noticed by people who came to Europe from abroad, such as the American critic Edmund Wilson who was in Naples in 1945. He sometimes thought that the Americans might as well take it over and make it into something which would be much better 'if only as good as Stamford, Conn.'. 'All these little sections, like Italy, why should anyone take them seriously?' he asked. 'Italy and Greece might be kept on as quaint and picturesque old places, as New Orleans is with us. The great mistake about Europe is taking the countries seriously and letting them quarrel and drop bombs on one another.' A Russian who also saw Europe from outside found herself disgusted with Europe. The European countries seemed small to the Russians, 'so cramped and so furiously nationalistic'. One realises how unusually courageous Saint-Simon was when he called for 'a European patriotism' to come into existence. He was writing in Paris in 1814, when the Russians had just entered the city and when the Cossacks were watering their horses in the Seine. Professor Agnes Headlam Morley was almost alone when, as Germany collapsed in chaos and destruction in 1945, she said, 'They are destroying Germany. They don't know what they're doing. They're destroying Europe.'

But even without the propulsion of public opinion behind them the governments of Western Europe continued to negotiate the co-ordination of tariff and monetary policies. It was decided to found a European market and an atomic pool. The European Economic Community came into existence on 1 January 1958, with France, Germany, Italy, Holland, Belgium and Luxembourg as founder members. It soon included a European parliament, a Council of Ministers, a Central Commission and a Court of Justice, as well as a number of agencies concerned with transport, investment, social funding and labour. It did not include Norway or Britain, which decided to try and torpedo the Community with the European Free Trade Area (consisting of Britain, the Scandinavian countries, Portugal, Switzerland and Austria). This was proposed to promote the liberalisation of trade and therefore make the

European Economic Community otiose. But EFTA was an ad hoc creation, while the EEC had a political rationale. Always within the EEC was the idea that Europe would, one way or another, unite; possibly, even, it included a potential federation which would be crowned by a supra-national authority. This would mean the end of Western Europe as a collection of nation-states, and the emergence in modern times of the first unified European government. There would be such a thing as a European identity: a *homo Europeanus*, a United States of Europe, an elected President of Europe, an edifice of Europe with agreed policies and procedures, a single European entity.

But there were difficulties in the way. The most obvious came from France and Britain. It was significant that the Community came into existence at the same time as General de Gaulle returned to power in 1958; he did not accept any reduction in the role of the nation-state or in France's complete sovereignty over her affairs, and he believed that any attempt to create a federated Europe would mean that it could become part of an Atlantic community dominated by the United States. For de Gaulle the United States was totally separate from Europe. Its economic, military and cultural power meant that it could dominate Europe, use it for its own purposes, corrupt its languages and culture, destroy the nature of the European nations. Shakespeare, Dante, Chateaubriand and Goethe, he argued, wrote in their own languages, not in some Esperanto or Volapük. It was therefore unthinkable to bastardise the nations by allowing them to dwell in the realm of some international ideology and technology. It was necessary to bring them into the realm of reality, that is to say, of politics. For de Gaulle, what counted was French supremacy; what de Gaulle's Europe needed was the anchor of a Franco-German alliance, forged through a de Gaulle–Adenauer understanding. Had not the Rhinelanders always looked to Paris as their cultural centre, and were not Rhinelanders especially susceptible to a Frenchman who was a general, a Catholic and a man with a sense of authority?

Of course many ardent Europeans claimed that this was an idiosyncrasy of de Gaulle, an elderly French nationalist more at home with the world of 1914 than in the 1960s. However, since de Gaulle retired in 1969 the same two principles have been retained by Frenchmen of all politics and generations. The Franco-German alliance and understanding has remained the focus of the Community. The fear that a European federation would become submerged in an Atlantic community has also persisted. 'The United States of Europe would become the Europe of the United States,' is the recent phrase of a leading French socialist.

The British position was more complex, more uncertain, more dependent upon circumstances. British governments did not expect the Community to succeed. They thought they could negotiate with the Soviet Union and persuade them to accept a reunited and neutral Germany in return for various guarantees; this failed. They believed that the Commonwealth would remain the mainspring of their activity, but they found that countries such as Australia and New Zealand were increasingly trading in the Pacific, that the new African and Asian states were drawn into local preoccupations with power and prestige, that the ties of imperialism had become mere attachments of sentiment, that the Commonwealth could not supply Britain's need for partners in any positive policy. They hoped that Britain was a privileged partner in an alliance with the United States, but they began to wonder whether they were not considered a diminishing asset.

In 1961 Britain entered into negotiations, belatedly, to join the Community. The application was vetoed by General de Gaulle in 1963 on the grounds that Britain was trying to maintain too many privileged conditions for the Commonwealth and would promote American interests, particularly in matters of defence. A subsequent application was also vetoed. A complicated and at times unedifying series of negotiations followed; Britain joined in 1973 and, after the unusual experiment (for Britain) of having a referendum, at last confirmed its membership of the Community in 1975. Ireland and Denmark had also joined in 1973.

This confrontation between England and France might seem to put in doubt the reality of a unified Europe. When General de Gaulle confronted the British Prime Minister, Harold Macmillan, they seemed hardly to agree on anything. According to Macmillan, when de Gaulle pronounced the word 'Europe' he meant 'France'. According to de Gaulle, when Macmillan was speaking of Europe he was thinking of an organisation which would have to accept the presence of a Britain which was jealously maintaining all its contacts and privileged relations with Commonwealth countries, and which was seeking to impose them on the other members of the Community. Macmillan described the difference in his own way. France, he claimed, was trying to resuscitate the Holy Roman Empire, which was centred on the Rhine. Britain, he said, was trying to resuscitate the Roman Empire, which had reached across the Channel and as far north as Caledonia. Where then was the real Europe?

The question becomes more complex still when one considers the other countries of the Community. The West Germans are primarily concerned with the division of their nation and are convinced that they must turn to the United States for their defence rather than to any European community. The Italians do not accept the rules. The Dutch do not like spending money on others. The Danes have the strongest anti-Market feeling of any state within the Market. The Irish claim that the Community is made up of their hereditary enemies. The Belgians are prepared to compromise on absolutely anything. The Luxembourgeois are only interested in housing, at some profit to themselves, the personnel of the community. The Greeks (who joined in 1981) are not prepared to cooperate. Spain and Portugal (who joined in 1986) have brought an atmosphere of controversy, typified perhaps by Spanish strawberry growers who undercut the prices of everyone else.

It is impossible to talk about the Community without talking about disappointments, failures and disillusion. It is always pointed out that the high hopes of the founders have not been met. There is no supra-national authority which can speak with one voice for Europe. There is no coordinated Western European policy on most international questions. The newspapers of the member states are essentially concerned with their own affairs, and Community matters are conspicuous by their absence. It never seems possible for the ministers to meet without a wrangle and a crisis, usually in monstrously long sessions. The budgeting of the Community is bizarre, and predictions of forthcoming bankruptcy are thick on the ground.

However, most serious of all, the Community finds itself at the centre of a moral dilemma. At the heart of the organisation there is a Common Agricultural Policy which pays farmers to produce in excess of demand. This gives rise to a popular antithesis. A well-fed and prosperous Europe – with a butter mountain, a wine lake and ludicrously high wheat, meat, milk and sugar production – struggles with the necessity of getting rid of unwanted surpluses, while, beside it, the Third World starves. All Western countries have seen television pictures of starving people in Ethiopia, Sudan, Mozambique and elsewhere in Africa. Everyone knows that in Asia or Latin America many children go to bed hungry and under-nourished. The European Economic Community can be seen as a white man's club, the hangover of an old selfishness, something of which Europe ought to be ashamed.

One argument in opposition to this antithesis is the agreement, known as the Lomé Convention, in which the Community provides aid and preferential trade agreements to some sixty African, Caribbean and Pacific countries. It has similar agreements with Central American countries, and bilateral arrangements with China, India and Brazil. There are provisions for food and emergency aid. It can be argued too that there are no developed countries with sophisticated political systems which leave their farmers at the mercy of market factors. Further, the farmers of the Community are constantly at odds over the trade in produce and the policies of subsidy: there has been no war in Europe, but there has been violence between national producers of eggs, lamb, milk, strawberries, early vegetables and other food. Still the fact remains: Europe is rich and food is overabundant, while other areas of the world are poor and desperately short of food. Members of Third World communities criticise Western Europe, often with great bitterness. Europeans, especially young Europeans, feel guilty and experience frustration too, because there seems to be no way in which they can remedy the situation.

The European Community has not evolved as many of its supporters expected. The 1960s was a period of prosperity which many now regard as a golden age, associating their nostalgia with the six nations unbesmirched by the presence of countries which are not fundamentally European, such as Britain and Ireland. In the mid-1960s, when there was a discussion about which countries might join the Community, the names that came up most frequently were Austria, Switzerland and Sweden. But none of these has joined. Once Soviet Russia had agreed to the restoration of Austria's national sovereignty in 1955, Austria was anxious not to be a geographical expression without prospects for a prospering economy and a free culture, and independence assumed a huge importance; Switzerland was anxious to preserve its neutrality; as was Sweden, within the Baltic enclave. The reasons for the states not joining the European Community are clear, but can one talk of Europe without Vienna, Geneva or Stockholm?

What then of Prague, Budapest and Warsaw, all European capitals? In Prague, at the Olsany cemetery, Russian graves are separated from the graves of the RAF, the Americans and the French. They are different in death. The Soviet Union for a long time sought to pretend that the Community did not exist, and tried to persuade their Eastern European clients not to enter into direct relations with the Community. This policy has started to crumble, but the problem remains that if Europe, as organised in an Economic Community, is to be more than a businessmen's arrangement, it must think of cultural relations with areas that are an essential part of its cultural heritage. This is all the more true because there is no cultural unity in Eastern Europe, despite its domination by Soviet Russia. Popular prejudice is as alive to this as a Frenchman is alive to the shortcomings of an Englishman or a Belgian. Someone from Prague will joke about the East Germans. We, he will say, have been fortunate enough to inherit from the old Habsburg Empire a happy-go-lucky way of life, a sense of incompetence and humour, which does not exist in East Germany. There the Germans are deadly serious. They take Marxism as earnestly as they took Bismarck, the Emperor William II or Hitler. In East Germany, it is said, communism is unbearable compared to Czechoslovakia; among the Czechs there was always someone who would help, someone who would make a joke, someone who would bend the rules according to the old tradition of the Austrian monarchy. Naturally the Germans do not agree, and have popular anecdotes to the contrary. Berlin, Prague, Budapest and Warsaw look back to different European traditions, though intellectuals in these capitals will claim that they are the most European of all. If you are born in Paris you can be Jewish or fascist or communist

or liberal, but you are automatically European. Since 1945, in
Eastern Europe you have to be quite exceptionally determined to
show that you are European and part of a civilisation which
stretches beyond the Iron Curtain, whose justification has little to
do with Europe itself.

The European Community is inadequate in many ways. Nevertheless it is remarkable and unique. For the first time since the
Reformation, Britain has made a peacetime engagement to the
Continent. For the first time in its history, France has opened its
frontiers to a large amount of outside trade. Italy, dissatisfied with
its own national history and conscious of a long series of failures,
has sought fulfilment in Europe. West Germany might debate
whether the atrocities of the Nazis were really worse than those of
the Russians and might ask if German history does not belong
to the Germans rather than to a pack of hostile non-German
commentators, but they are able to defend themselves all the better
because they are Europeans. Belgians seek to drown the divisions
between Flemings and Walloons by being European. The Dutch
revel in the fact that they are the best linguists in the Community
and that the organisation gives them the best framework for their
famed national obstinacy. Ireland is able to reduce its links with
Great Britain. Denmark remains loyal to the separateness of Scandinavia while having a profitable foothold in Europe. Spain has
resolved the age-old debate about whether Europe begins before
or beyond the Pyrenees. Luxembourg has demonstrated that a very
small state with a population of just over 100,000 can exercise
considerable influence. The Greeks have found that membership
of the Community allows them to play an independent role in
world affairs. Portugal has emerged from a long period of isolation.

But naturally this round of achievements is not necessarily agreed
upon by all the inhabitants of the member-states. It is impressive
to count the number of meetings which are held every week in
Brussels, Luxembourg and Strasbourg. Ministers, commissioners,
ambassadors, officials, experts, members of the European Parliament, trade unionists, representatives of special interests are constantly in touch, as are heads of government. But this is precisely
what the general public finds boring. The Community appears to
be an intensely bureaucratic body, constantly meeting in order to

produce a mountain of regulations, many of which are incomprehensible to anyone who is not in the magic circle of the initiated. The British public remembers rumours about London taxicabs being abolished since they did not conform to the standard taxi that existed elsewhere, and about how British (and Danish) chocolate could not be called 'chocolate' if sold in the Community because it contained a quantity of non-cocoa vegetable fats. They remember stories of how often dramatic and ill-tempered scenes occurred in meetings of chief ministers, usually with Mrs Thatcher fighting for a rebate on Britain's contribution to the Community budget or demanding an overhaul of the Common Agricultural Policy. In all these matters the Community appears either boring or ludicrous, and not only to the general public. One can understand what James Callaghan meant when he said that on becoming Foreign Minister he had to start a fresh round of negotiations with the Common Market, but he decided instead that 'the time had come to cultivate the rest of the world once more'.

Yet though the Community may seem an arid organisation, a population has emerged in the thirty years of its existence which feels itself to be very European. Other prophecies have proved unsuccessful. England has not become the Sicily of Europe, poor and cut off from the mainland; according to the Eurobarometer which conducts opinion polls of the member-states 48 per cent of British people do not think membership has brought economic benefits, 66 per cent are against leaving. Community countries have not become hideously Americanised, or lost all sense of a European identity, though an enormous McDonald's has appeared in one of the most prestigious squares in Rome, and famous cafes and restaurants are being replaced by fast-food shops, and distinctive styles are disappearing in favour of uniform plastic. These signs are superficial. As a French magazine put it, 'Blue jeans reign from Sicily to Denmark, but nowhere do they rule.'

When President Heuss of West Germany made an official visit to London in 1958, the crowds lined the streets and watched the Queen with her guest. But they did not applaud. Most people remembered the war, or the discoveries which were made in its aftermath. Although they knew that they could not justly blame this particular man for what had happened (and they may well have had German friends, and been far from hating or reproving all Germans), they could not bring themselves to applaud the symbol of Germany. But already there was a younger generation which did not think this way. When young people rebelled against their parents over how they should dress and how they should cut their hair, the war usually came into the argument. 'It's not so much that we're told that when our fathers were our age they had to have short back and sides in the army, it's rather that it seems that they won the war because they had short back and sides,' was one complaint. Generations grew up for whom the war was over. Before the Community made frontiers the simplest of formalities, the world of pop music, casual clothes, football, films and cars had already abolished frontiers. Those who idolised the Beatles or who flocked to Swinging London were not interested in stories about 'perfidious Albion' or songs like 'We Are Marching Against England'. Football commentators had to learn foreign languages in order to inform their audiences about foreign teams. Football fans took to travelling. Students took it for granted that they would go abroad, and schoolchildren expect foreign travel to be organised for them.

The last forty years or so have been a period in which, to use a sociologists' expression, 'the people have entered society'. This is not only a matter of tourism, although the difference is immense between travel today and travel before 1939. It is a matter of identity. More and more young Europeans, if questioned, will say that they are European; more and more feel free from the confines of nationalism and national histories. Other subjects have come to interest them, and have replaced questions about who was responsible for the war or why one army was victorious. Nor are they necessarily enthusiastic about any national political party or the religion of their country. It seems unusual for a young French person to hate Germans or for an Italian to be hostile to Greeks. There is instead the desire to be entertained and the desire for enjoyment. There is an interest in people, often accompanied by concern for the old and the handicapped which would have been unlikely some years ago. There is a concern for the environment. There is the expectation that they will be looked after in sickness or in unemployment. There is a shared cynicism when faced with authority or with authoritarian pronouncements, and this means not only a cynicism about parents but also about the superpowers, the United States and Soviet Russia. As far as big causes are concerned there is a certain listlessness. The patriotism of the modern German is not 'Germany over all', but that Germany is the centre of Europe and that Europe is the centre of the world, no matter what they say in Washington or Moscow.

Of course this is only a small section of the population. Perhaps a favoured section, the 'Euro-yuppies' or the 'Aufsteiger' who seemingly flourish in a continent racked by unemployment, or perhaps a more disreputable section, the football hooligans who originated in Britain but who have found imitators in France, Spain and Italy. At all events one is talking about a decreasing section of the population, since it is estimated that with declining birth-rates one in five Europeans will be over the age of sixty-five by the year 2000. In any case, it is unwise to generalise too much about a generation, since change can be disconcertingly rapid.

But one can notice a growing moral self-consciousness in Europe which does coincide with many of the preoccupations of the young of today and yesterday. We pass laws against racist behaviour, laws about making environmental changes even if the land is privately owned, laws to prevent birds' eggs being taken from the nest or badgers being baited, laws against sexism, laws about discrimination and many more in a long list. Even when there are no laws there is an expression of concern about such matters as nuclear waste, the slaughtering of seals, lead in petrol, additives in food, factory farming and many others which vary from the eccentric to the deadly serious. These laws, projected or wished-for, do not simply protect the social fabric at the expense of limiting the freedom of the individual. They positively try (to use Jane Austen's phrase) to screw the citizens into virtue.

Yet Western Europe's capacity to arrive at this comparatively progressive condition is limited, limited by the way in which it is over-arched by the superpowers. Europe has always refused to be ruled by one state; when Hitler made the last attempt, he was frustrated by the force of men and arms from the United States and the Soviet Union. However bravely the national flags fly, the parades roll past and the anthems blare, Western Europe knows that she lost her pre-eminence with the war and will not get it back. The First World War started the slide and the last war accelerated and confirmed it. Whatever the wealth and power of the twelve nations of the European Community, whatever its future technological and economic developments, the continent which once dominated the world now lives under the military and economic shadow of two superpowers. The modern reality is that the fate of Europe can be decided by these powers, one of them the most prosperous 'open society' that the world has ever seen, the other the most powerful, closed, collective society the world has ever known. The economy of Europe is to a large extent dependent upon that of the USA. The centre of gravity of world trade is moving from the Atlantic to the Pacific, the revival of prosperity in Western Europe is dependent upon the revival of the American economy, the value of the dollar, and the extent of American protectionism.

This is made all the more complicated by the democratic process as it exists in America and by the political system of the Soviet Union. The President of the United States may be the most powerful man in the world, but recent history has shown only too clearly that his power may suddenly be curtailed. This does not mean that American democracy is in turmoil, but that as the President grows weaker Congress grows stronger, until there is a Presidential election and the process is reversed. When Gorbachev arrived on the scene in Moscow it had become accepted wisdom that the Soviet Union was a conservative gerontocracy unable to reform itself. It is not easy to predict how extensive or how permanent the change that has been initiated will be. But what is certain is that Europeans have been bystanders while the Americans have gone into one of their periodic periods of introversion, and the Soviet Union has launched a new initiative to achieve dynamism and gain influence on the world stage.

A second limitation imposed upon Europe derives partly from its imperial past. At a time when numbers of people are thinking of themselves as Europeans, many immigrant or minority groups do not agree. A young coloured girl in Brixton says, 'I'm English, because I was born in England, but I'm not European.' Other immigrants, even second- or third-generation, would not go this far. Some Afro-Caribbeans wish that they knew the language of their ancestors, so that like the Asians they would have an identity which did not depend simply upon the colour of their skin. In areas like Liverpool, Bristol and Birmingham one can see the development of an inner-city culture which does not depend upon Britain, and has even less to do with the continent. Some four centuries after their ancestors were forcibly removed from Africa in the slave trade, many young Afro-Caribbeans, through Rastafarianism, dancing or drumming, are trying to rediscover their African roots.

In France, although most of the North African communities have undoubtedly settled in France for good, there remains a certain nostalgia for the lands which they still regard as home, and to which they cherish the secret hope that one day they will make enough money to return. Now that Islam is the second religion in France after Catholicism – and there are more Moslems than Protestants – there is a widespread demand to see Islamic law recognised by the French state. There seems little possibility that the Mahgrebin population will be assimilated into the French.

Much the same can be said of the two and a half million Turks who live in Europe (one and a half million in West Germany alone). Should Turkey become a member of the Community (and the Turkish government officially made the request on 14 April 1987), the presence of an Islamic state in Europe, one which will probably have a larger population than either France or Germany by the end of the century, could fundamentally change the notion of being European.

Yet some minority groups see a solution to their problems in emphasising their European nature. The Euskara-speaking Basques are divided into seven different regions, three north of the Pyrenees and four south. They refuse to consider themselves Spanish; many of them are reluctant to consider themselves French. They are Basques first, and *Europeans* second. Similarly, it was a celebration of the tenth anniversary of British and Irish entry into the Community, held in Belfast in 1983, that provided the first occasion since partition for a Prime Minister from Dublin to make a speech in Northern Ireland.

Thirdly, Europe is over-arched by its history. Europe is a guilty continent. Two photographs would be enough: one of war graves, one of Auschwitz. There may be young Germans who do not know who Hitler was; there are Frenchmen who claim that the gas chambers never existed; many say that the figure of six million Jews murdered in the Holocaust is exaggerated. But it is impossible not to consider these events as the greatest of crimes, and this is how they are seen by Africans and Asians. Many Westerners must feel a sense of alienation from their ancestral civilisation. Age-old Europe was a place of death and destruction. This can be forgotten temporarily, but the memory can never be destroyed. The West's civilising pretensions are betrayed by the Holocaust, and this seeming hypocrisy has assisted in the rejection of the European concept of human rights. How can the West speak of human rights, or of individual right? In organisations of the United Nations such as UNESCO there is an emphasis on collectivism, the demand that an individual conform to the ideas of the state and become part of the unified mass.

When the United States withdrew from UNESCO in 1984, they made several charges against it. One was the allegation that UNESCO had become 'statist', allowing the rights of a modern collective society to override the rights of the individual. This implied that traditional cultural practice should have priority over the claims of an individual conscience. In contrast to the United States, the Soviet Union upheld statism.

Here are two examples. First, if individual women, or groups of women, in states where female circumcision is practised object to this ritual, they are likely to be told that it is part of traditional cultural practice and that it is the declared duty of the state to uphold it. Second, the Third World countries called for the establishment of a journalist's code of good practice, complaining that Western journalists were not reporting Third World affairs objectively, but sensationally. To Western eyes such a code of conduct meant restriction of their freedom; had it been implemented, it would have struck at a fundamental Western principle, the right to report what one sees.

The UNESCO debates illustrate the weakness of these Western principles. Journalists' claims for objectivity and freedom can sometimes hide a blinkered self-indulgence. In any case, one of the most powerful professional exports from the West to the Third World today is persuasion: the art of public relations which serves capitalism, television programmes which keep the masses quiet – politically above all. It is not the real values of the West – the rights and duties of individuals – that are being defended.

For Europeans there is a danger that the traditional and precise sense of the rights and duties of the individual is being replaced by a rootless 'individualism'. This can be both a freedom and a burden. Individualism can become a prison, and the tenets of a purely individual morality can be a lonely burden, lost, without a sense of history, progress or purpose.

The question is asked: is the West going anywhere? Perhaps the West has deceived itself. Its law is not universal. Even in Europe tolerance of the slow compromises that are needed to make democracy work is questioned and rejected. Sometimes rejected in favour of 'direct action', a corrupt euphemism for violence; sometimes simply neglected altogether. Perhaps Western values are not always secure even in the West itself.

The library, Pannonhalma monastery, Hungary 'Those who cannot remember the past are condemned to repeat it' (George Santayana)

7 · THE INCOHERENT CONTINENT?

An English historian, Dr Peter Burke, has recalled standing one day in the main square of Cluj, in Transylvania, looking at a nineteenth-century statue of King Matthias Corvinus. Groups of tourists were taking photographs of one another in front of the statue, and all were speaking Hungarian. For Hungarians he was 'good King Mátyás', a Magyar of the Magyars, and the city they were standing in was called Kolozsvar. But to the Romanians the city is Cluj Napoca, within the boundaries of Romania, and Matthias is a Romanian. These confusions are frequent in Central Europe.

The Hungarians have a tenacious historical memory. They recall 'historic Hungary', much of which ceased to be Hungarian in 1919, becoming part of Romania, Czechoslovakia or Yugoslavia. The writer Istvan Bibo has talked about 'the wretchedness of the small countries of eastern Europe', which have had their frontiers changed frequently but which have never had frontiers corresponding to linguistic boundaries. He quotes someone saying, 'I was born under the monarchy, I spent my childhood in Czechoslovakia, I began my family in Hungary, and now I live in the Soviet Union.' 'Well,' said another, 'you must have travelled a great deal.' 'Oh, no,' came the reply, 'I've never left the town where I was born.'

The novelist Lajos Grendel, a Hungarian living in Czechoslovakia, expresses the historical memory of his community. His identity, like theirs, incorporates a commitment to the present and a nostalgia for the past, the immediate and the historical. If the actors change, the scenes are always the same: suffering, massacre, denunciation, heroism, betrayal. There are always masters, and it makes no difference whether they are Turks, Austrians or the Communist Parties of today.

Milovan Djilas, the Yugoslav dissident, wrote a novel about Montenegro. It begins with Montenegrans, in 1916, facing the army of advancing Austrians; it is about a society which is dissolving and which will only be resurrected in memory. Montenegro takes pride in its own identity and hopes for a future in which Serbia will transform that identity into a free Slav state. A young man has a love affair with a girl from his village. He is a supporter of the greater Serbia, she refuses to give up her belief in the old Montenegro. When they find that their love affair is becoming serious they run away from each other; thus Montenegro takes leave of itself and of its past. The novel ends in the new Yugoslav state, where the old warrior feuds and the old Balkan dreams seem petty, foolish and meaningless.

Ismael Kadare is an Albanian who was born in 1936. He is old enough to have known those who remembered their country being governed by the Turks. In an occupied country, he says, it is culture that takes the place of a university, a parliament or an academy. Children learned about their history by listening to the talk that went on around them, and Kadare delves into this cultural tradition with his novels about the First World War.

These novels should not be called historical novels. They are novels about history. They exist for people who have lost their cultural roots, and now look for them and need them. There are many peoples in Europe who have powerful memories for the past because they need to rediscover or hang on to their roots. The Irish are an obvious example. Wolfe Tone, Robert Emmett's speech from the dock, the Great Famine, the Easter Rising of 1916 are living memories. If today statisticians tell us that Irishmen marry later than men in other states of the European Community, it is because the recollection of an Ireland where poverty postponed marriage and family is still present. If young Irish men and women caught up in the present crisis readily leave Ireland in large numbers, it is because they are still part of the tradition whereby the Irish emigrated overseas in their millions.

Poland, too, has a powerful past. Perhaps Poland needs its historical memories because it is there that Europe begins to come to an end; it has not known the religious wars, the French Revolution, the Industrial Revolution, and it has known communist revolution only by the process of forceful implantation. Even Poland's Catholicism is said to be passive – that is to say, faithful, obdurate, proud, but not part of the creative, evolving Catholic Church (in this respect it is comparable to Irish Catholicism). The memories of Poland's past have always inflamed the conviction, through the ages, that Poland would 'rise again'. Andrzej Wajda's film *Ashes*, set in the Napoleonic era, provoked national controversy about the role of the Polish legion in Napoleon's armies. The visitor will be shown the roads which the French army took in 1812 during its invasion of Russia. Napoleon himself is the centre of a great moment of Polish historical romanticism. He was the Emperor from the west, who dominated Europe, who created the Duchy of Warsaw, who fathered a Polish son, who attacked Russia. The Polish insurrection of 1944 against the Germans is seen in the perspective of many other risings, both before and later. The reconstruction of Warsaw after the war meant the restoration of the old city, stone by stone, a remarkable physical assertion of the strength of Polish nationalism.

Hungary, Montenegro, Ireland, Poland are among the vanquished of history. They must relive their history in order to resuscitate it, to visualise it, to reflect on how it might have been different, to manipulate it, to glorify it. But this is not so in other European countries. It is often said that recorded history is a success story because it is written by the successful. In *The Education of Henry Adams* one reads, 'Society is immoral and immortal; it can afford to commit any kind of folly and indulge in any sort of vice; it cannot be killed, and the fragments that survive can always laugh at the dead.' The successful can afford to forget the past because they do not need it, or they can display the past as a spectacle, a show of magnificence, a source of entertainment. But in such cases the past provides neither inspiration nor inhibition; it is merely something which seeks applause and which receives a temporary interest.

For most Englishmen the past exists in terms of ritual. Of course we know that Englishmen trailed their pikes across France, that Drake beat the Spaniards, that Wellington beat Napoleon, that Englishmen died in the trenches of the First World War, in the Battle of Britain and in the D-day landings. (At least, earlier generations knew this; it appears that many of the present generation do not.) But the most vital link with the past is embodied in the British royal family. The Coronation, the Trooping of the Colour, the service of remembrance in Whitehall, all these are part of the pageant which claims to re-enact the history of this country. Even the Queen's broadcast each Christmas Day is part of a ritual, with its references to the Commonwealth recalling the past, even if the tradition of the broadcast is recent. But none of this directly explains or critically discusses history. Just as the historical plays about Henry VIII or Elizabeth I which are shown on television rarely mention a date, so the presentation of British royalty is not connected with the issues of British history. The ceremonial is intimately linked with the life stories of the members of the royal family – their marriages, careers, children, state of health, duties, leisure, privacy – so that we are seeing not the unravelling of distant ages so much as the most glamorous soap opera of our time. The fact that so many other countries which have little or no connection with this royal family are also riveted by the slightest event concerning these real people confirms the unreality of this supposed vehicle of historical memory.

It is difficult to say whether or not England has a national hero. Stories about King Alfred are often repeated and his statue can be seen in his capital, Winchester; Queen Elizabeth I has her partisans; Cromwell has had streets and hills named after him, as has Wellington; Churchill epitomised British heroism at a crucial moment of history (though so did Chatham, Pitt and Lloyd George, none of whom seem to run in the national hero stakes). But there is no agreement on any of these figures. There would be more support, curiously enough, for Nelson, although Trafalgar Day is no longer commemorated. Perhaps the most support would go to Shakespeare; the fact that his birthday coincides with St George's Day, the patron saint of England and the Order of the Garter, is significant. But, outside Stratford-on-Avon, no one celebrates this day. Shakespeare is probably the best known of Englishmen but this is not the same as being a national hero. And St George, saint and knight-errant, supposedly born in the third century in Cappadocia (now Turkey) but also said to have been born in Coventry and to have slain his dragon in England (Warwickshire, Berkshire and Herefordshire all lay claim to the site of this feat) is not a convincing English hero.

If England has no national hero, then France suffers from having too many. Leaving Charlemagne on one side, there is St Louis, Joan of Arc, Louis XIV, Napoleon, Clemenceau and de Gaulle, plus many regional heroes. History also plays a more important part in the life of France than in that of Britain; the notion of French greatness and some sort of French superiority is associated, however vaguely, with the grandeur of Louis XIV's court, the military victories of the French Revolution and the heroism of Verdun. French history tends to be popularly remembered as victorious (in contrast to English history which often commemorates heroic unsuccess, like Captain Scott, who was second in the race for the South Pole, or the evacuation of the British army from Dunkirk in 1940).

East Germany has found it necessary to emphasise its historical origins, and to explain that the Democratic Republic owes its existence to the age-old peasant and worker tradition of the German nation, the peasant revolts of the Middle Ages, the revolutions of 1848, and even to such figures as Luther, Frederick the Great and Bismarck. But this is a deliberately manipulated history. In West Germany there are those who claim that it is necessary for a new history to emerge if the Federal Republic is to find direction signs to its identity. Germany, it is said, can exist as a sovereign state, but it cannot exist without the German nation. Therefore a history must come into existence which will lead Germans out of the trauma of Nazism, the war and the Holocaust, and establish a consensus among themselves. What is required is a German history fit for the Germans of today. And many historians would say that this is precisely the task which cannot be performed to order.

When Bonaparte decided to make himself the Emperor Napoleon in 1804 he appointed a commission to choose an imperial emblem. Various animals were considered, such as the lion and the elephant, but the commission was keen on the cockerel, since its Latin name was 'gallus', which has the same root as 'Gaul'. But Napoleon scorned the idea since, as he said, the cockerel was too weak; it was for the farmyard and could not represent a strong empire. Eventually the eagle was chosen. Then a personal emblem was necessary. Napoleon, conscious of the need to find roots as far back as possible in the past, heard about the metal bees that had been found in the tomb of a sixth-century Frankish king called Chilperric, and thought that this emblem would link his empire to the pre-Capetian dynasties. But neither emblem has persisted in the consciousness of France. The imperial eagle and the bee are meaningless as symbols, and it is the cockerel which is recognised, although most French people who feel entitled to crow like a cock ('Cocorico') at some sporting success would be hard put to explain why. Manipulated history is not successful.

If history does not seem to have much meaning in many Western societies, this could be the fault of historians. Like all academic disciplines history, in Western Europe and in America, has become highly specialised and professional. This is not new. In the eighteenth century Fontenelle wrote, 'To fix in one's head facts, to settle dates exactly, to fill oneself with the spirit of wars, treaties, marriages, genealogies, that is what is called knowing history. I had as lief a man acquired exactly the history of all the clocks of Paris.' But now, adding to this complaint that historians can be arid and pedantic, we have the increasing availability to the historian of the most sophisticated statistical and numerical techniques. Voltaire's warning, 'Woe to details, they are a sort of vermin that destroys big works,' has never been more relevant.

If history is to become part of individual life, it must impinge upon the young. Yet for young people the past is alien to the environment that surrounds them. It is difficult to see it as part of a continuing stream of events within which their family and friends exist, or as part of their hopes and ambitions for the future. There are societies in which myths and legends about the past do involve the young. The consciousness of speaking a different language from other cultures may give an indelible impress of the past, affecting both the present and the future. This happens in Eastern Europe and it happens among many immigrant communities and minority groups wherever they are to be found. But in the majority of Western countries history appears today as either a series of intellectualised abstractions seeking to establish patterns and laws in history, or a concentration on the collection of detail and the praise of complexity. There is little connection between the past and the present.

It is easy to say that the past has gone, that the past is dead. The old landscapes have disappeared, the old communities have broken up. To study the past is to investigate a world that we have lost, to sample the wealth that has vanished, to visualise those things which might have happened but did not. It can sometimes come down to contrasting the riches of the past with the ugliness of the present.

It is not surprising that one way in which Europeans connect the present to the past is actually to resuscitate the past. Museum-making could be the third biggest growth industry in Europe (after accountancy and office development), and there seems to be no topic or theme which is not worth museum treatment. If outsiders from Europe, especially Americans, consider that many parts of Europe constitute a museum anyway, then this is not inappropriate.

An annual prize is given for the best museum in Europe. In 1986 it was given to a Dutch open-air museum on the edge of what was once the Zuiderzee, which has long since been sealed off by a dam. Years have been spent on the careful recreation of an old-style Zuiderzee fishing township, with faithful reconstructions of canals, boats and windmills, with shops selling the biscuits, cakes and sweets of the time. This reconstruction of a past community is a popular form of museum activity. There is a big open-air museum in Beamish, County Durham, and one just outside Belfast with isolated nineteenth-century houses, a schoolroom, a small line of terraced houses, a church, workshops and a mass of lovingly assembled period objects. A village museum in Bucharest seeks to do the same for a large and heterogeneous peasant community, while in western France it is common to come across Breton farmhouses and manor houses which have been kitted out as museums to attract the passing tourists.

These reconstructions are usually admirable and well-patronised. But what do they mean to the many people who visit them? Do the visitors recapture some sense of their roots as they look at earth floors, primitive sanitation, peat fires, unrecognisable tools, crowded living quarters, strange advertisements? Of course it gives pleasure, especially to the elderly who come across things from the past which they can perhaps dimly remember. But this is a nostalgia for one's youth, a curiosity about the day before yesterday. If, for the professional, history has become the pursuit of erudition, for the museum-goer it has become a diversion. It is not a part of one's being, transmitted through the experience of the family, the community or the school.

It is interesting that museum-going is so popular. Perhaps groups of people like the simple process of contemplating objects together. The objects need not necessarily be objects of the past; one of the most successful museums to have been created in recent times is the Pompidou Centre in Paris. It has many features which are practical and useful, such as a library and a collection of films and cassettes. There is no attempt to reconstruct any feature of the past as in a folk museum, but obviously the enormous collection contains many objects of the past. The whole project – which brings together a totality of cultural objects, such as books, paintings, sculpture, film, furniture, either in permanent collections or temporary exhibitions – was very ambitious, but now that it has been in existence for more than ten years its extraordinary success can be seen. An average daily attendance of about 7000 was expected, but something like 24,000 people have attended each day. With seven and a half million visitors a year the Pompidou Centre has easily outstripped the Eiffel Tower (which has three million fewer). Yet what is the point of this vast assembly of disconnected objects? Some claim that 10 per cent of all visitors walk through the centre without looking at anything in particular. It is a spectacular

example of consumerism, with visitors looking largely unpercep-
tively at a bewildering variety of displays and going away satisfied,
having consumed a few aspects of culture. It is the physical equivalent of a 'cultural' television programme. It is also a remarkable
example of how a wealthy European country ostentatiously
demonstrates its wealth.

Along with the museum craze goes the craze for anniversaries,
which is often justified in terms of the need to teach history. Official
anniversaries are, as has been discussed earlier, a part of the
paraphernalia of the nation-state. It is natural too that those who
have served together in some battle will want to come together
again on the anniversary of that battle, especially if it is an anniversary which seems special in terms of years – the tenth or the
twenty-fifth, for example. But there is little justification for many
organised anniversaries. In 1987 the authorities of Paris have
decided to celebrate the fiftieth anniversary of the International
Exhibition which was held in Paris in 1937. One wonders whether
they will, in ten years' time, celebrate the anniversary of the
celebration. The care with which organisations, newspapers and
individuals seek to discover anniversaries, is another sign of a
desire for contact with the past.

We have to assume that this contact with the past has been
lost in Western Europe because of the speed of change. The
disappearance or the transformation of so many of the values and
assumptions which made up Western society has made the past
seem irrelevant. Through the savagery of recent years we have lost
touch with the world behind us. It is difficult, if not impossible,
for Western Europeans to visualise a world without organisations,
such as clubs, libraries, tourist offices, good food guides, Sunday
newspapers, cinemas and television companies, which provide for
one's leisure time. There are historians who can, with learning and
patience, discover what men who worked from sunrise to sunset
did in their moments of rest. But the search for evidence is severe
and depends upon erudition. The result will be published in a
specialised review and will have no impact. The alternative is to
consider the problem as part of an entertainment, whether in a
film or in a museum, and once again this has no impact on the
viewer, it is separate from him as *voyeur*.

Doubtless historical explanations have too easily been proved wrong. 'History is an old whore,' said Goebbels in his last broadcast before committing suicide in 1945. It is not the fault of history that history was not on the side of the Nazis as Goebbels and his associates had presumed. 'If we are defeated we will slam the door of history behind us,' Goebbels also said. But the reader of history who discovers the assumptions of the past and who considers the many predictions concerning progress, peace, equality, justice, nations, democracy, class which were put forward may well consider that the past has been devalued. The reaction against traditional historical studies, while not obviating the need for historical roots and a connection with the past, has been a reaction against ideology.

Western Europe was accustomed to having a section of society which thought in terms of ideology, defending established institutions and values and proposing new ones. This section was the intelligentsia, the intellectuals. Intellectuals have traditionally been more important in some countries than in others (in England, for example, where prior to 1914 few assumptions were called into question, the role of the intellectual was always limited, though England's commitment to the world beyond Europe assisted in the creation of a powerful school of anthropologists). In France the intelligentsia were always important, and the influence of French intellectuals has been felt in a great many other countries.

Yet it would seem that a strange silence has come over European intellectuals. There has not been a major European intellectual movement since the Existentialism which flourished after the Second World War and the Marxism which persisted into the 1960s. The former, preoccupied with freedom and the individual, was always in confrontation with Marxism and was soon dominated by it. Marxism, suffering from its associations with the Soviet Union and from a disillusionment with the evolution of the communist world in general, developed into a series of academic exercises. Later movements such as structuralism tended to be closed, professional movements isolated in academic jargon and which belittled men's initiatives, efforts and aspirations. What was the use to men of philosophies which sought to get outside manmade history?

Did the war disturb European self-confidence more than we have recognised? Most Continental nations had the bitter experience of surrender, occupation, betrayal, the evidence of moral capitulation as well as of heroic resistance. Disputes still exist about the guilt of those who fought, about resistance movements, concentration camps, gas chambers. Though England did not experience occupation, there were long years of fighting, a realisation of the loss of power, the understanding that there would be no return to the world that existed before 1939. Too many questions have been asked about the war and all its implications. Intellectuals began by giving too many answers, answers that could not satisfy. In the West they ended by giving up.

The Peruvian novelist Mario Vargas Llosa has said that artists, writers, intellectuals are treated better and given more prestige in Eastern Europe, Latin America and the Third World in general than they are in the West. If they associate themselves with the government in power and devote their talent to supporting it, they are treated like princes. If they are dissidents, they have a sense of mission and a purpose for their activity, although the price may be high, too high for most intellectuals of the West.

In Western Europe there has recently been a new tendency to express ideas in action, to try to live out change rather than simply to express it in intellectual terms. Thus one learns little about the philosophy of education, but much about computer technology, accountancy, engineering, electronics. Environmentalists are interested in doing things first, rather than discussing legal rights or theories of law. Devotees of Eastern religions want to practise their faith in their communities and on the pavements of the cities rather than indulge in theological discussion. Schoolteachers will go on strike in the name of educational priorities rather than enunciate the principles of this education. The emphasis is on problem-solving rather than on ideas.

Regional and ethnic minorities have discovered the importance of history, and they use it in practical ways. As the majority grows distant from the past, these groups discover or imagine their own past, and on the basis of these discoveries demand special considerations and rights, often in language and education, but sometimes in terms of the economy and investment. They may suffer repression, as the Albanians of Kosovo in southern Yugoslavia did in 1981 – in which case another incident is added to their historical memory and to their cherished legends.

Twenty years ago when students in Paris, Frankfurt, London and many other Western cities initiated revolutions and indulged in violence they could claim that they had intellectual masters who had taught them what to do. In Germany the Frankfurt Institute for Social Studies, with Professors Adorno, Horkheimer and Pollock, had explained the sordid inefficiencies of capitalist society. Elsewhere, Marcuse and the Canadian professor McLuhan had urged that the young needed roles, not goals. A hundred years earlier the anarchist Bakunin had argued for 'a contagious passion of youth' in the hope that it would turn into general rebellion. Acts of violence have long been seen as resistance against crimes of exploitation. Every day on the factory floor, it was said, violence is committed against the workers. Morality and metaphysics, it was claimed, had been invented in order to keep the millions quiescent. Therefore violence was justified intellectually, even if the acts of violence themselves seemed unrecognisable to the supposed mentors of the rebellion.

But more recently, Western European countries have experienced a totally non-intellectual, irrational version of violence, in the aggressive hooligan, criminal and racial violence which can be found on public transport, or sporting occasions, in the cities. Although some countries experience this more than others, it is a Western European phenomenon which can only be explained by the disintegration of the traditional codes of discipline, whether those of the family, the economic and social community or sporting groups. Violent films such as the *Rocky* and *Rambo* series, films of action and imagery without ideas, messages or lessons, are also an influence. A haphazard, pervasive and meaningless cult of violence has developed.

It is here that one should discuss attitudes to religion. When we talk about Europe we are, after all, talking about an ensemble which is historically closely linked to organised religion. If values in Western Europe are shared, if people of different nationalities speaking different languages have similar perceptions, it is likely that these are based on deep-rooted cultural experiences which are built out of lasting social influences. The Christian religion is an outstanding example of an agency which has sought to create common values and beliefs throughout Europe, and which has always had a profound social significance. In a recent survey of ten Western European countries (Greece and Portugal were the two which were excluded from the twelve states which now make up the Community) it was found that church attendance, denominational affiliation and belief in orthodox Christian doctrine (Catholic, Protestant or Nonconformist) were all in decline, especially among young people. These findings allow for many variations, since women demonstrate significantly more religious inclination than men, since farmers and fishermen tend to be more committed to religion than either skilled manual workers or the unemployed. Further, there does seem to be some sort of religious disposition, the recognition of a religious need or the existence of some sort of spiritual experience, among a relatively extensive section of the population. It is as if the formal, ritual, historic side of Christianity is less easily accepted, while the more personal, intimate and irrational elements of religion remain widespread among large numbers of Europeans. If the overwhelming majority, even of practising Christians, rejects the idea that there are absolute guidelines about right and wrong to be derived from religion, there remains a general adherence to certain moral precepts.

Many changes in attitude have occurred in recent decades; the widest fluctuations have been in the pattern of sexual relations and the family. This has been mediated to the boy and girl in the street by a complex set of public arguments, of which feminism is only one. Fertility has become a matter of choice because of advances in medicine. Social attitudes have caused law reforms so that the incidence of divorce has risen, accompanied by a rise in second marriages. There are institutions besides the family to care for the young, the old or the handicapped. Economic conditions have facilitated marriage, and in the 1960s one grew used to the idea that people would marry at increasingly early ages, the 'child bride' of tradition being matched by the 'child groom'. Sociologists said that such youthful marriages were a sign of revolt against parents. But the idea is now widespread that marriage is not necessarily the normal result of a love affair. Surveys in France, for example, suggest that while 60 per cent of young people believe in romance and a romantic commitment to a partner, less than 20 per cent believe in marriage (the nature of this enquiry is so vague that statistics are bound to vary considerably). In the past the inevitability of legal marriage was not always accepted, especially in the working class (in England, for example, during the First World War, it was necessary to introduce special arrangements so that the many common-law wives and their children could receive pensions and compensation when their common-law husbands or fathers were killed or wounded). But by the inter-war period, marriage was the norm for young people, and it is this that has changed. There was a time when Western Europeans used to look to Scandinavia as the area where experiments in living together (what the French call a *'mariage à l'essai'*) were common and unlike anything that existed in other European countries. If Scandinavian habits seem to be extended into Western Europe, one must distinguish between living together as a preliminary to marriage (or remarriage), and living together as an alternative to marriage (the latter is widely accepted in the Netherlands, for example).

In Western Europe as a whole, and in Eastern Europe as well, the institution of marriage is not outdated. Marriages may be broken by divorce, which is accepted and regarded as normal. Sexual tolerance and acceptance of premarital sex is widespread; the single parent family has become common; the right of children to develop with their own autonomy and dynamism is accepted. But the institution of marriage remains, and close families with mutual obligations between parents and children, with a sharing of attitudes between partners, persist. How this pattern will change in the future is difficult to envisage. Marriage retains a meaning, a hold and a reality, as well as some sort of symbolism. Like all social institutions, it has always been adaptable.

We are told that we are entering an age of leisure. If that is so then the puritan work ethic is likely to dissolve. Most Western Europeans spend a major part of their daily life in paid employment; for most of them, work is the focus of their lives. Researchers have found that workers are concerned about the intrinsic content of their jobs and the ways in which they provide opportunities for initiative, as well as about the security and rewards which they seek and require. But the same research also shows a pre-occupation with the 'pleasantness' of the occupation. The sight of an assembly line in a motor factory, or of any mechanised and automated work process, is enough to explain why physical work has lost its savour. It has been reduced to the machine-like tending of machines, which is very different from the management of domestic animals or the exercise of human dexterity in manual work.

Thus people are ready to move into the leisure society, without having a work ethic, without having a sense of history, guidelines of behaviour or belief, or much imagination about the future. Conceptions of the future used to be shaped by conceptions of the past, by the accretion of values and dogmas transmitted from generation to generation. This heritage is being liquidated as we move into the servicing society, the mass communications society, the plastic card society, the society of endless pervasive and persuasive words and pictures. This is a society which brings everyone together in a momentary unity, at the level of some TV programmes and via, say, frozen foods; but it is a society which also stratifies, as TV programmes are aimed at different consumer levels and frozen foods divide into cheap takeaways, gourmet packs and levels in between. There are more and more subdivisions, the modern substitutes for the divisions of social class, but with no hereditary aristocracy at the top there are many rights and few duties. European satellites will widen this process and internationalise it. There will be programmes in many languages, with precisely-timed spots for the international advertisers. The great multi-language international mass-advertisement will be born. Societies concentrate more and more on the present, with nostalgic glances at the past and only uneasy thought for the future. The media provide the daily opium; bureaucracy ensures smoothness.

As a result, the continent which has always had an elevated sense of the past and has prided itself on its consciousness of its roots, which has always had visions and ambitions for the future and which has prided itself on being creative, now increasingly fulfils Tocqueville's nightmare of disconnected individuals living in a tutelary state. One has to ask whether there is still – above or below the level of the huckster, the salesman, the politician, the bureaucrat, the makers of soap-operas – any European coherence intellectually, imaginatively, creatively. One answer comes from Czechoslovakia. The dissident and exiled Czech writer Milan Kundera has written about 'a kidnapped West', and about culture bowing out. The idea of Europe, he says, is dying.

Czechoslovakia is a key to Europe. People sometimes laugh at Shakespeare for providing Bohemia with a sea-coast in *The Winter's Tale,* but there was a brief time in the thirteenth century when the rule of the Bohemian king stretched as far as the Adriatic. This king was Otakar Premysl, who ruled from 1253 to 1278, and who anticipated the Habsburg Empire by several centuries. Because Bohemia was placed in the field of gravity between Pope and Emperor, its rulers had always veered from one to the other. Nowadays Czechoslovakia is placed in the field of gravity between Western and Eastern Europe.

Kundera has protested that the movement of liberalism known as the Prague Spring which was suppressed by Soviet tanks in August 1968 is too often compared to the student revolts of May 1968 in Paris. The latter, he claims, challenged European culture and traditional values, but the so-called Prague Spring was a passionate defence of the European cultural tradition in the widest and broadest sense. It was as much a defence of Christianity as it was a defence of modern art, since both were equally denied by the authorities. Those who took part in the Prague Spring, according to Kundera, were struggling for their right to the European tradition, which they saw as being threatened by the anti-Western Messianism of Russian totalitarianism.

But now, living in the West, Kundera like other Czechs asks if Europe has lost all sense of direction and purpose, or if it is living in the delusion of an authority it no longer has. Is the continent which developed and proposed to the world the splendid ideas of individual rights and free speech now quite unable to grasp how far and how fast those ideas are disintegrating across the world? Believing that the history of the novel is a mirror of man's history, Kundera names the three greatest twentieth-century European novelists as Proust, Joyce and Kafka.

These are the three novelists usually selected by orthodox communist East Europeans as those novelists who have led the novel off the right track (they were particularly attacked at the Cultural

Congress which was held in Leningrad in 1958). But he distinguishes between them. Proust and Joyce, he claims, lived in the assurance of the pre-eminence of the individual. He could have enlarged upon this, with Proust lying in his cork-lined bedroom at 44 rue Hamelin, a nocturnal creature of pure fantasy, whose external existence had almost ceased to matter; with Joyce choosing to be an exile, sustaining his quarrel with Ireland all his life so as to give force to his artistic vocation. But Kafka, according to Kundera, realised that meaningful personal lives could no longer be lived with assurance. He sensed the imposed collectivism – which is not a community – which characterises the Soviet Union and the Eastern bloc. 'No more solitude. The idea of Europe is dying. It is the end of Europe.'

Thus Western Europe has to save itself for its own sake. It must also save itself for the sake of Europe as a whole. For many the problem is that each nation is absorbed in its own present, defending its own benefits rather than its own values or virtues, at best letting rationalism conquer the intuitive. The exiled Polish poet Czeslaw Milosz, who has a mixed ethnic background, mocks the national strife which occurred, and which in a way still occurs, between Poles and Lithuanians over one particular town. 'The Poles maintained,' he writes, 'that Vilno should belong to Poland, the Lithuanians that Vilnius has always been and would be part of Lithuania.' If today someone calls the capital of the Lithuanian Soviet Republic Vilnius, he suggests a Lithuanian identity; if he calls it Vilno, Lithuanians will assume that he is Polish or Russian. 'Perhaps,' comments Milosz, 'those sardines fighting each other in the mouth of a whale are not untypical of the relations between humans when they search for self-assertion through ethnic values magnified into absolutes.'

What is hoped for, in some quarters, is a fading away of the state. People of many different nationalities and political ideas have been seeking this and predicting it. The institutions of the European Community were originally intended to help states fade gracefully and voluntarily, so that from being a customs union the Community would move into being a defence, foreign affairs and political union. This move would fall into the tradition of post-war settlements – The League of Nations, the Permanent Court of

International Justice and the International Labour Office were formed after 1918, and the United Nations and its fellow organisations were formed after 1945. Membership of these international bodies would, it was thought, lessen the self-assertiveness of states and promote cooperation between them.

This was all the more likely to happen because the power of a state, in the contemporary world, is no longer dependent upon the possession, or protection, of sovereign territory. The folklore tale of two states fighting each other to the death for the possession of a small piece of valueless land, the name of which is soon forgotten, is no longer relevant. Power is derived from economic, technological and scientific resources.

Yet these expectations have not been met. The power of individual states over their societies and economies has not been loosened. What has been called by Eastern Europeans 'the proverbial self-centredness' of Western Europeans has flourished within the Community, and when Community agricultural ministers argue over milk quotas they are like Milosz's sardines fighting in the whale's mouth. And statesmen still behave as if land were the basis of power. The Soviet Union forcefully resisted any modification in the systems of government in Hungary (1956), Czechoslovakia (1968) or Poland (1981) which might weaken its occupation of Eastern European territory, and has sent its troops into Afghanistan in order to forestall a possible internal political change which would allegedly weaken its frontier. The United States evolved a policy of containment whereby the Soviet Union should not be allowed to extend its territorial limits, and has fought wars in South Korea and Vietnam to prevent the expansion of what it considered to be Soviet client-states. Great Britain fought a war in the distant Falkland Islands in order to preserve its sovereignty. France has sent troops into Chad in order that African states should respect certain (imaginary) frontiers. In Berlin a wall marks a frontier and the four occupying powers maintain token forces in that city.

But it would not be true to say that nothing has changed. Increasingly one is aware of the economic power of transnational corporations. Their capital and their control of technology give them the capacity to influence the structure of production within a national state. Increasingly too one is aware of competition for technology in defence matters. International affairs are necessarily dominated by those *political* entities, which have substantial scientific and technological resources at their disposal. The individual states of Western Europe are not large enough to be able, individually, to organise the capital or the technological or scientific wherewithal to compete or to keep up with the superpowers. The message is, and has been for some time, that the Western European states, and to begin with those which form the European Community, must combine to overcome their particular vulnerabilities. Otherwise they will become, industrially, dominated by the United States and Japan and, in defence, dependent upon the United States or defenceless before the Soviet Union.

There has been a response to this dilemma. The industrialists of Europe have formed an association called the Group of Twenty-two comprising the twenty-two leading European transnational corporations, which funds new ventures in advanced technology, organises access to markets and influences governments to act positively in terms of taxation, benefits, contracts and research. The hope is to give a new impetus to Western European industry. But the concern of this group is not only with Western Europe, but also with the Third World and the industrial development of some of the territories there. The French government, faced in 1984 with the United States's Strategic Defence Initiative, which sought to devise a highly advanced technological defence system against the delivery of nuclear weapons, hastily launched a rival research programme for defence called Eureka. This would involve the whole of Western Europe and would prevent European scientists from contracting to work for the American programme. Whatever the doubts about the effectiveness of SDI or the feasibility of constructing something similar, the idea of a European counter-project would prevent the United States from capturing European scientific resources.

The European Laboratory for Particle Physics, sometimes known as CERN (Centre Européen pour la Recherche Nucléaire) is an example of a common European scientific enterprise. It is based in Geneva, and its site stretches over the Franco-Swiss border. It is funded by some fourteen European countries and has a staff of

3500; its laboratory resources are used by several thousand scientists from all over the world, but mainly from Europe. Within this organisation nationalities disappear, and there is no system whereby the nationals of any one country are granted facilities which only correspond to the funds which their particular country has invested in the project. The cost of this complex of accelerators and their operation, the use of large visual and electronic particle detectors and the extensive data processing facilities, would be well beyond the resources of any single European country no matter how prosperous. Over the last few years a considerable new project has been launched, the construction of the Large Electron Positron Collider, which will have important scientific and industrial implications.

CERN admits to financial problems, and in order to develop its new project it has had to close down certain fields of research. Nevertheless, for twenty-five years it has provided the sort of large organisation which is necessary for research in particle physics and it claims not only to have stopped the brain drain of scientists to America but, on occasions, to have reversed it.

The European space programme which expects to satisfy Western European demands for telecommunications and observation satellites also hopes to participate in the first human Mars landings, not long after the projected American landing in the year 2020. The European space budget is only one-sixth of that of the United States, and the number of European scientists working on the project bears no comparison with the half a million Soviet technicians and scientists who are similarly employed. However, it is an important, combined European effort. Grand technological programmes are not the only means whereby the modernisation of a society can be measured; there are also economic benefits in view. But more particularly, it is argued that if Europe does not take part in the most exciting adventure of our age, the exploration and the domestication of space, then our continent will have become not merely historically ancient but intellectually old. Europe is the continent in which modern science started its long tradition. It can play, in all realms of science, a vitally important role among the great powers.

Another dramatic example of the determination to make the

coherence of Europe work is the close and, as some call it, privileged partnership between France and Germany. The enemies of three wars have become the hinge of the European idea, as typified in the bustling city of Strasbourg. This partnership is all the more remarkable because it is difficult, much more difficult than most observers credit. The didactic streak in the German approach to European affairs which has led them to regard their own handling of economic affairs as the *Modell Deutschland* for others to follow, their dependence upon the United States for defence, their reluctance to distance themselves from Israel in Middle Eastern affairs, their sensitivity to the idea that they have been the paymasters of Europe, all this has not been easy for the French to handle. The French insistence on the Common Agricultural Policy, their hostility to the anti-nuclear movement in Germany, their doubts about Germany's future diplomatic intentions, their impatience with Germany's insistence upon carefully maintaining good relations with the small states of the Community, have all posed problems for successive West German governments. Yet in recent years there have been scores of detailed changes affecting the nature of Franco-German relations. German visitors to France can withdraw money from their savings accounts at French post offices. Customs formalities for private citizens travelling between the two countries have been abolished. The domestic telephone market has been opened to both French and German firms in the two countries. And along with these and other schemes, there was the emotional and powerfully symbolic ceremony in September 1984, when Chancellor Kohl and President Mitterrand stood side by side at Verdun, commemorating the dead of their two countries in the most terrible of battles.

Something of the European ideal is being realised. The national idea, the idea that the inhabitants of any one country have only one overriding duty, to push forward the interests of their own particular state, is on the wane, if only because of the new framework within which decisions have to be taken. The idea of forming a coherent and autonomous Europe, too weak (in comparison with the superpowers) to become aggressive but too strong to be overawed, is making progress. Further major moves which are due to take place in 1992 will make the Community more united in economic terms and will undoubtedly increase the powers of the European Commission in Brussels (by the Single European Act).

Of course, cynics will say that ministers always promise more than they give, that there is little midway between the empty rhetoric of politicians and the Commission's daily production of word-mountains which threaten to match the mountains of butter, beef and cereals which overload Community stores. You do not have to be very cynical to distrust the Commissioners, who are not elected, sitting in a plate-glass monstrosity on a hill near Brussels' triumphal arch, disguising hard economic facts with accounting devices. It is all the easier to be cynical in England, which has remained marginal, only enthusiastic when prophesying budgetary disaster and resentful when taken to task by the European Court of Human Rights.

No one can say whether or not the Franco-German friendship will last for ever. Some have the nagging worry that what Nietzsche called Germany's 'hidden paths to chaos' may be lurking underground, or that the forces of French nationalism may be revived by some political or economic crisis. No one can say whether or not the emergence of a sophisticated and technologically orientated Western Europe, increasing the gap that lies between its countries and those of Eastern Europe, is in the longterm interests of Europe as a whole. An ecologist would argue that the problems of natural resources are common to the whole continent: the forests of both Western Germany, from the Schwarzwald to the Bayerischerwald, and Bohemia are threatened with destruction. An economist would argue that an economic crisis is also common to the whole continent, with unemployment and areas of arid poverty as the hallmark of the West, and shortages of goods and stagnation as the hallmark of the East. The technological and commercial uniformity of the West is coming to rival the political and economic uniformity of the East.

Yet diversity exists. East Germany exults in its claim that it has no Nazi past for which it should feel guilty, because communism was always opposed to the Nazis. The Poles fiercely maintain their identity. The Czechs look to the West. The Romanians claim that when the head is bowed it is not cut off.

The diversity of the West is its most striking characteristic; it is this which a French sociologist, Edgar Morin, has defined as the outstanding originality of Europe. He describes a number of contrasts and dialogues: empiricism versus rationalism, the particular against the general, philosophy and science, religion and reason, faith and doubt, myth and critical thought, Hamlet and Prometheus, Don Quixote and Sancho Panza. A German writer has recently commented that the Nazi war criminal Mengele was as European as Michelangelo.

The whole can make for incoherence. But it can also make for coherence and for an idea of Europe, a continent that is more than a continent, and which is much needed by the rest of the world.

INDEX